DELAYED REPLAYS

a collection of comic strips by LIZ PRINCE

DELAYED REPLAYS © 2008 LIZ PRINCE
Published by TOP SHELF PRODUCTIONS
p. o. box 1282
Marietta GA 30061-1282 U.S.A.
Publishers ♡ Brett Warnock & Chris Staros ♡

TOP SHELF PRODUCTIONS ® and the TOP SHELF logo are registered trademarks of TOP SHELF PRODUCTIONS.

visit www.topshelfcomix.com   and spend generously
Cover colours by Maris Wicks
1st printing, May 2008. Printed in Canada, eh.

This book is dedicated to everyone who stars in these comics with me. If you are one them, please write your name here: _____

This book is also dedicated to everyone who has complained about not being in one of my comics. If you are one of them, please write your name here: _____

THANK YOU.

breadsicles for my love

Liz Prince 2005

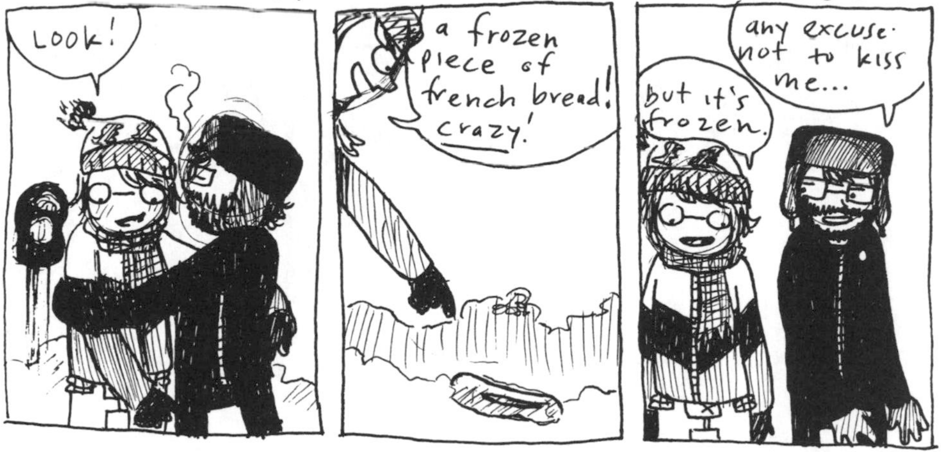
Look!
a frozen piece of french bread! crazy!
but it's frozen.
any excuse not to kiss me...

The cars are buried

LIZ PRINCE 2005

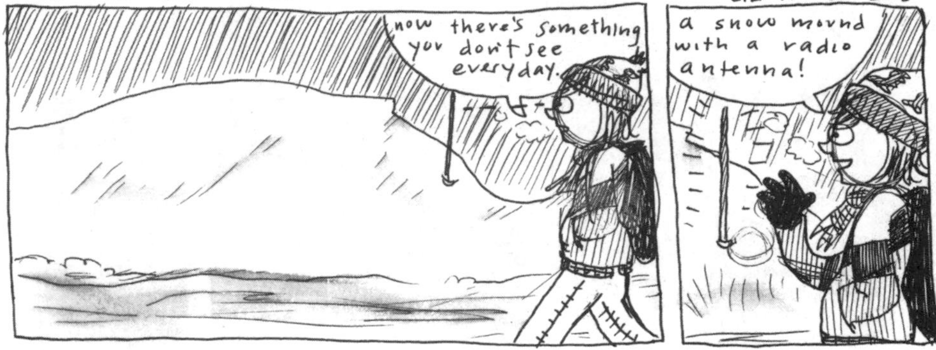
now there's something you don't see everyday.
a snow mound with a radio antenna!

kitten self-defense

LIZ PRINCE 2005

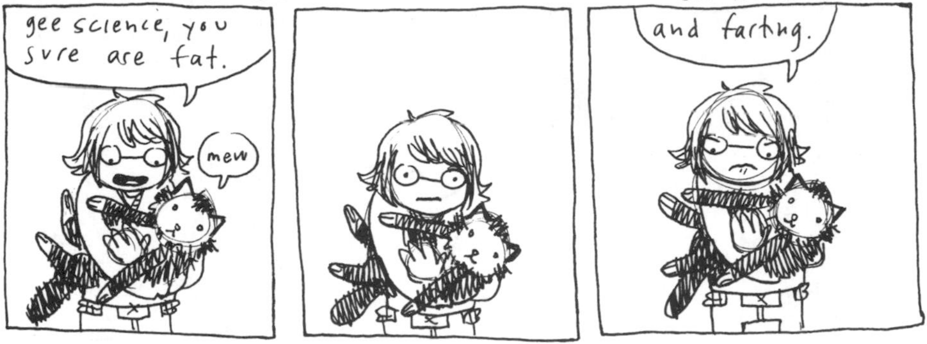
gee science, you sure are fat.
mew
and farting.

whack-a-doo

LIZ PRINCE 2005

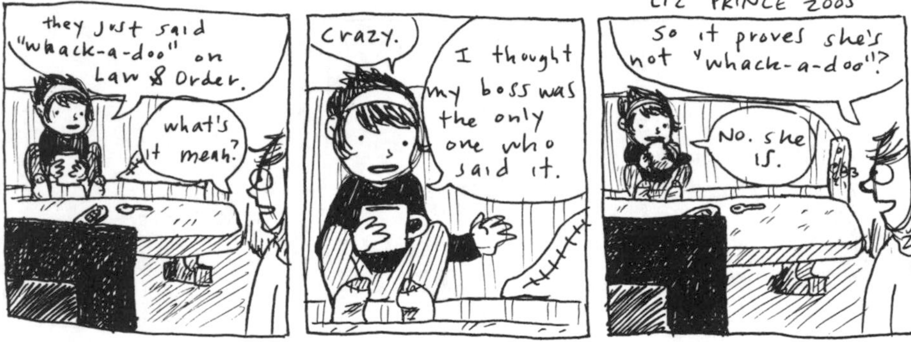
they just said "whack-a-doo" on Law & Order.
what's it mean?
crazy.
I thought my boss was the only one who said it.
So it proves she's not "whack-a-doo"!?
No. she is.

making a mixtape.

LIZ PRINCE 2005

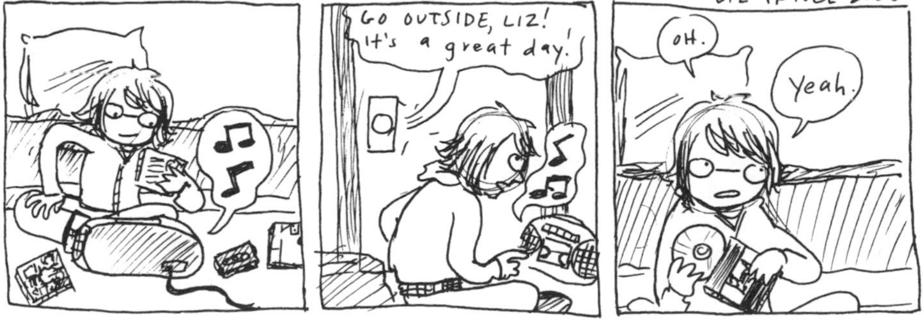
GO OUTSIDE, LIZ! It's a great day!
OH.
Yeah.

piggles

LIZ PRINCE 2005

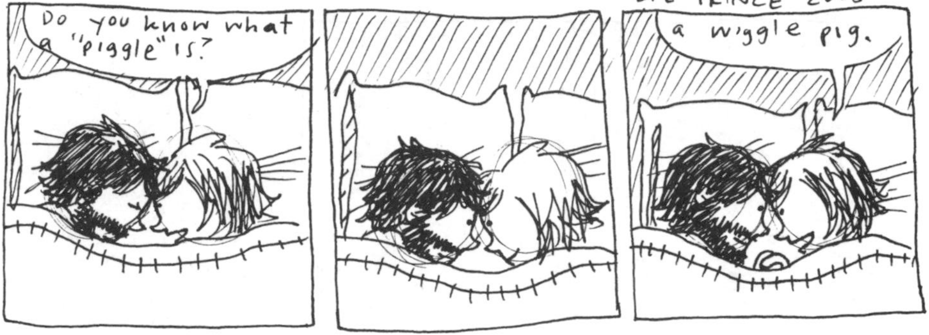
Do you know what a "piggle" is?
a wiggle pig.

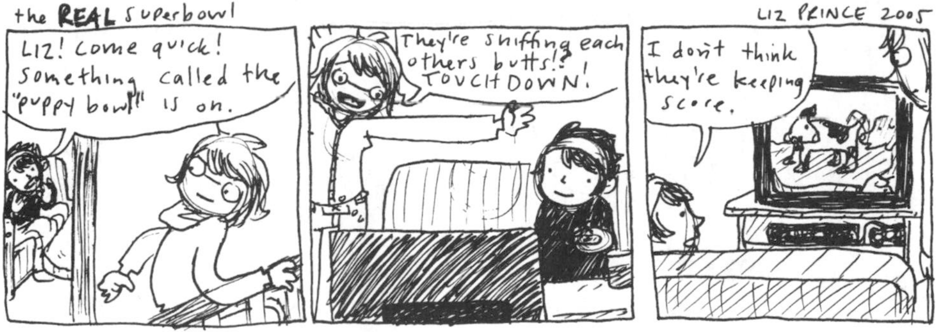
the REAL superbowl
LIZ PRINCE 2005
LIZ! Come quick! Something called the "puppy bowl" is on.
They're sniffing each others butts!? TOUCHDOWN!
I don't think they're keeping score.

the death of homeless Jesus

LIZ PRINCE 2005

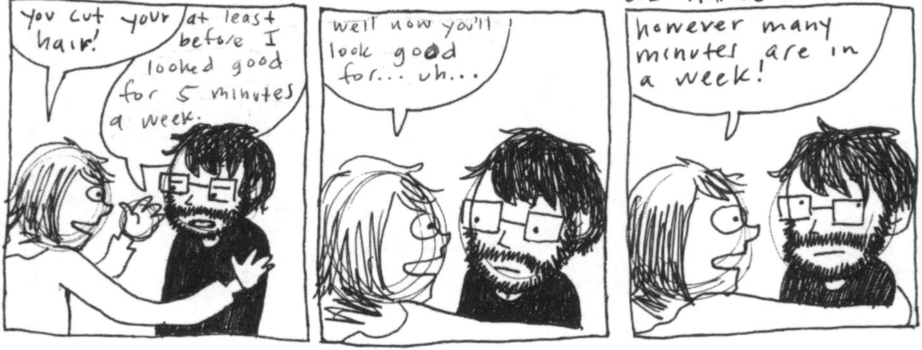
you cut your hair!
at least before I looked good for 5 minutes a week.
well now you'll look good for... uh...
however many minutes are in a week!

How fucking romantic

Liz Prince 2005

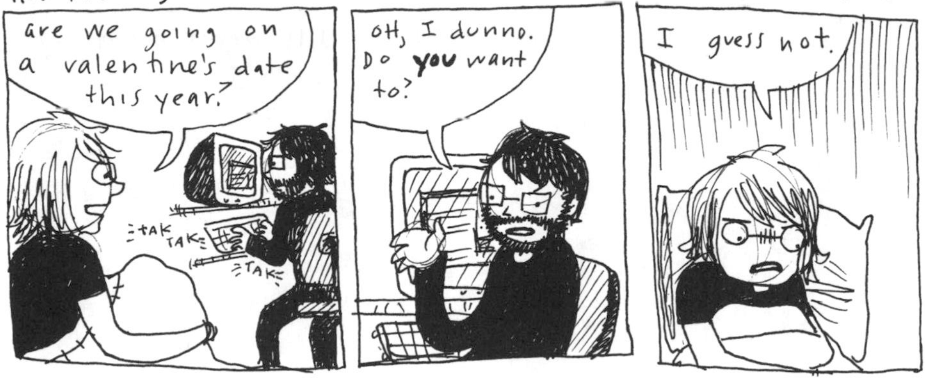
are we going on a valentine's date this year?
TAK
TAK
TAK
OH, I dunno. Do **you** want to?
I guess not.

Stupid

LIZ PRINCE 2005

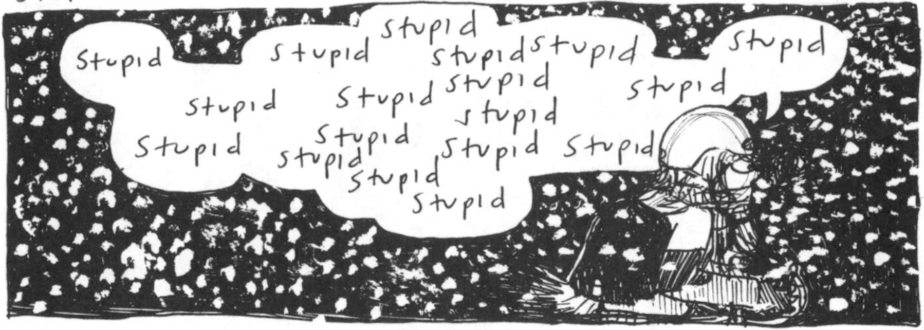
Stupid stupid stupid stupid stupid stupid
stupid stupid stupid stupid
stupid
stupid stupid stupid stupid
stupid
stupid
stupid

grapes of wrath

LIZ PRINCE 2005

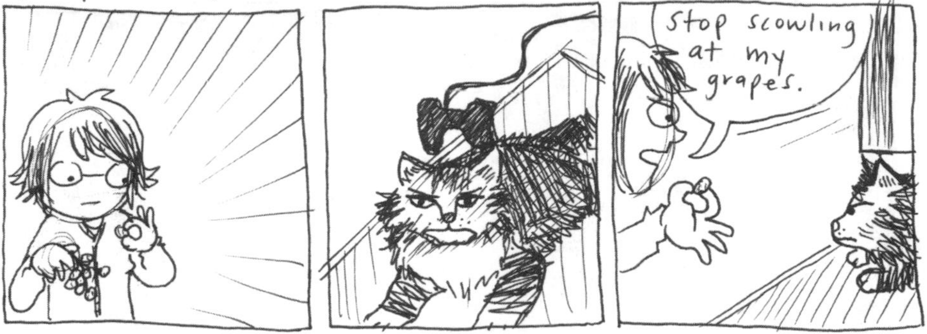
Stop scowling at my grapes.

Feelings

LIZ PRINCE 2005

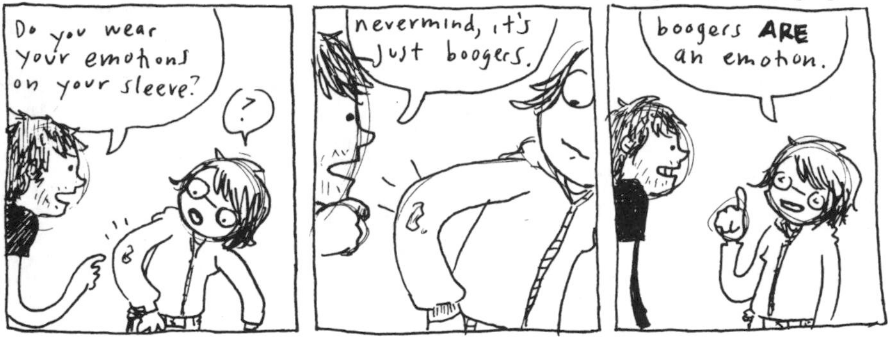
Do you wear your emotions on your sleeve?
?
nevermind, it's just boogers.
boogers ARE an emotion.

the best valentine EVER.

LIZ PRINCE 2005

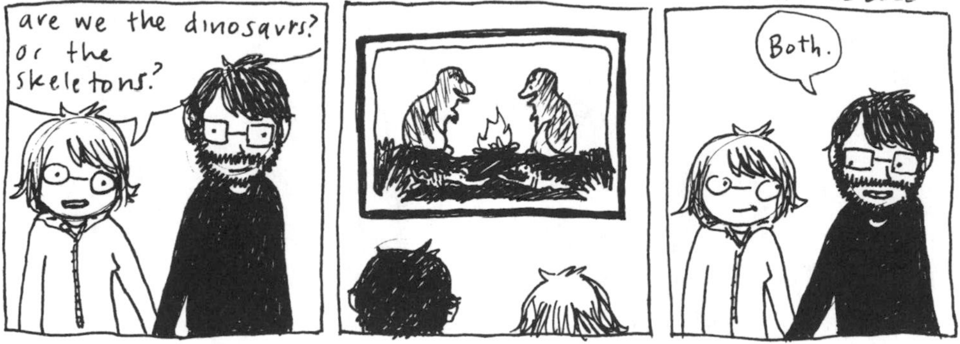
are we the dinosaurs? or the skeletons?
Both.

danmccarthy.org

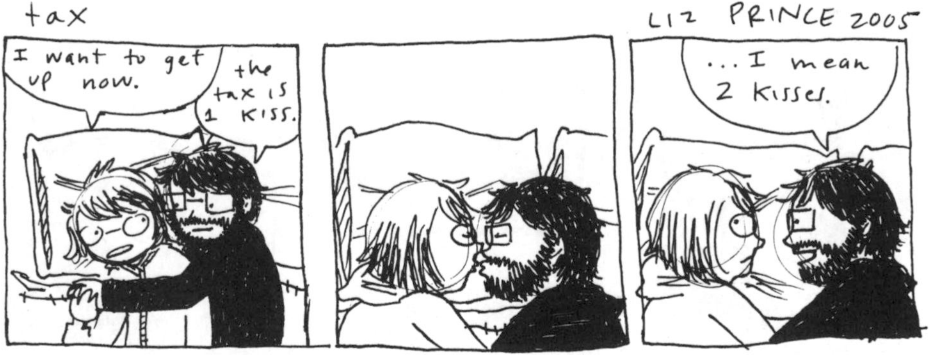
tax
LIZ PRINCE 2005
I want to get up now.
the tax is 1 kiss.
...I mean 2 kisses.

science diet

LIZ PRINCE 2005

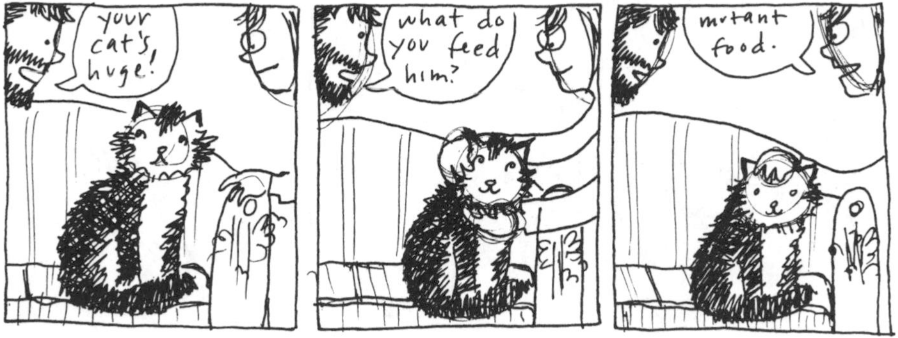
your cat's huge!
what do you feed him?
mutant food.

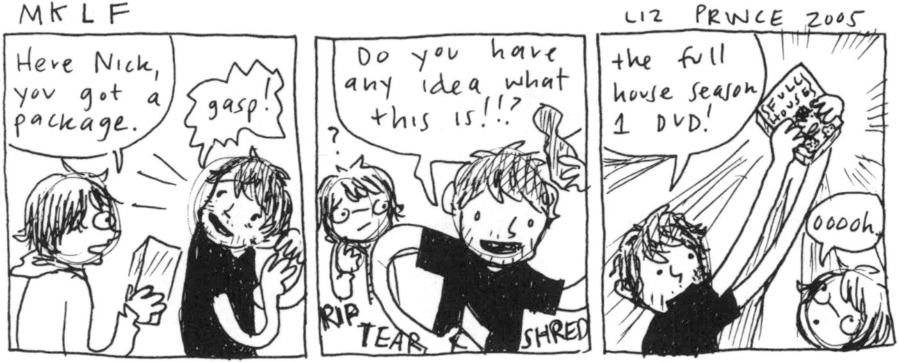
MKLF
LIZ PRINCE 2005
Here Nick, you got a package.
gasp!
Do you have any idea what this is!!?
?
RIP
TEAR
SHRED
the full house season 1 DVD!
FULL HOUSE
ooooh.

stupid sulk

LIZ PRINCE 2005

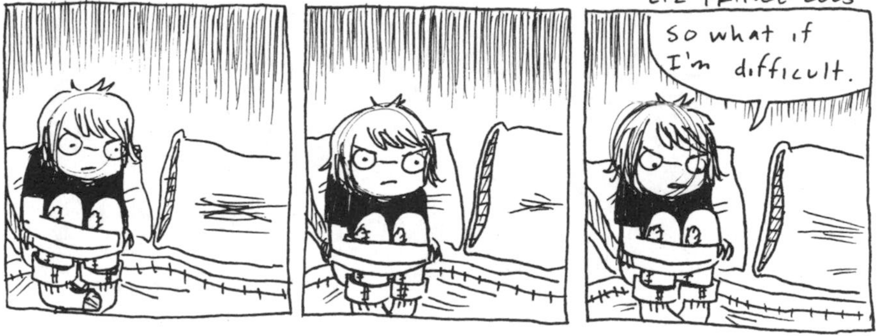
so what if I'm difficult.

Katamari Combat

LIZ PRINCE 2005

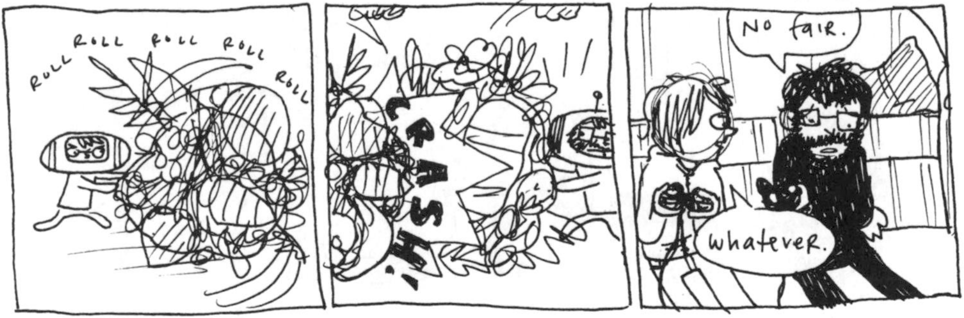
ROLL ROLL ROLL ROLL ROLL
CRASH!
No fair.
whatever.

Late night cram session

LIZ PRINCE 2005

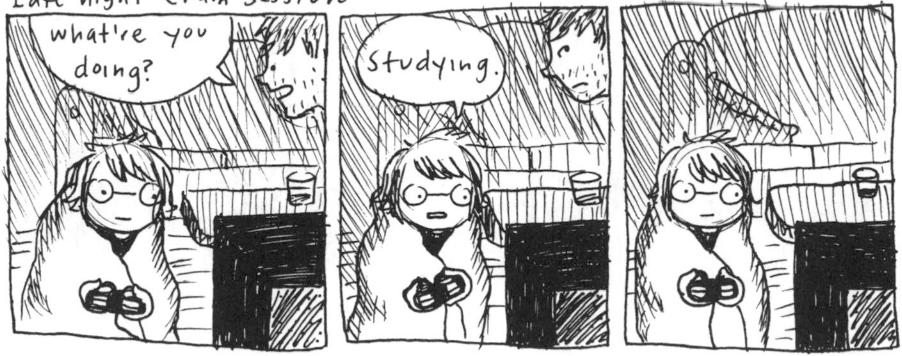
what're you doing?
Studying.

Studying for real

LIZ PRINCE 2005

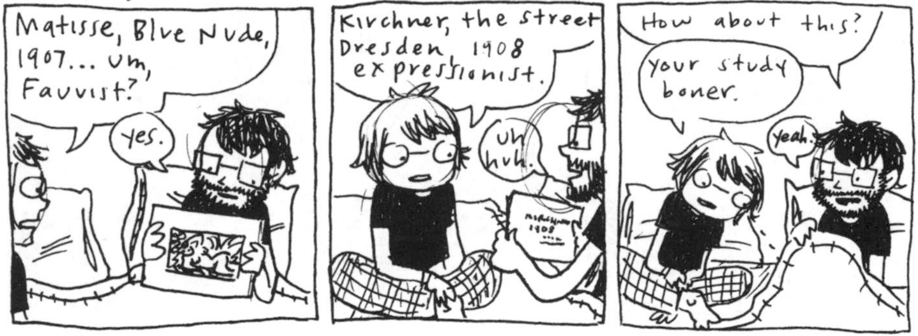

Matisse, Blue Nude, 1907... um, Fauvist?
yes.
Kirchner, the street Dresden, 1908 expressionist.
uh huh.
How about this?
your study boner.
yeah.

true ghost stories

LIZ PRINCE 2005

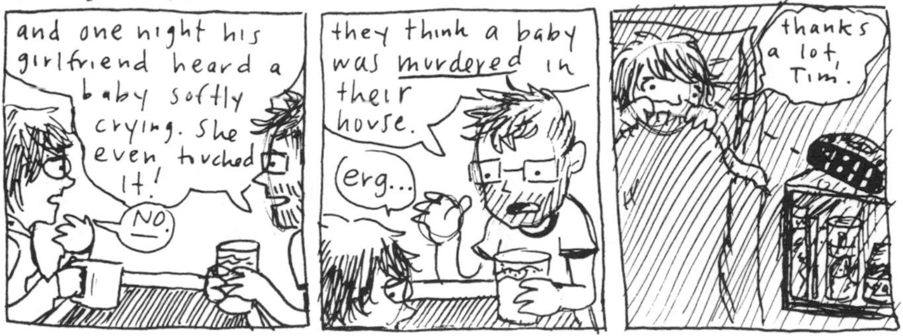
and one night his girlfriend heard a baby softly crying. She even touched it!
NO.
they think a baby was murdered in their house.
erg...
thanks a lot, Tim.

cat talk LIZ PRINCE 2005

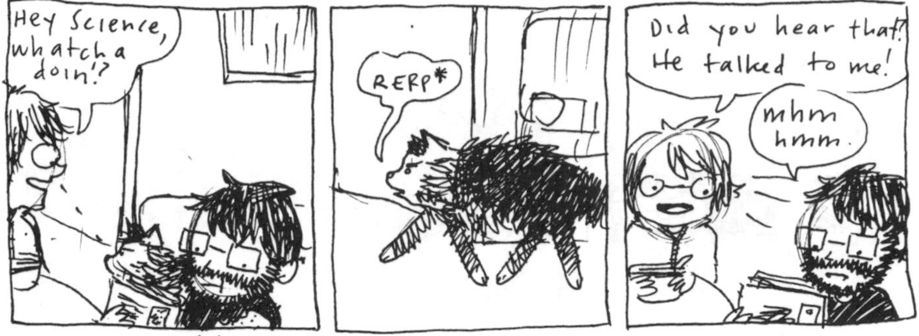
Hey Science, whatcha doin'?
RERP*
Did you hear that? He talked to me!
mhm hmm.

*"I am going to poop on the floor."

bedtime

LIZ PRINCE 2005

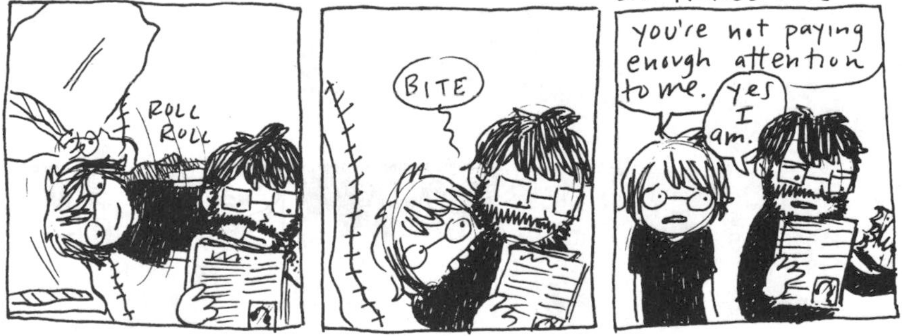
ROLL
ROLL
BITE
you're not paying enough attention to me.
yes I am.

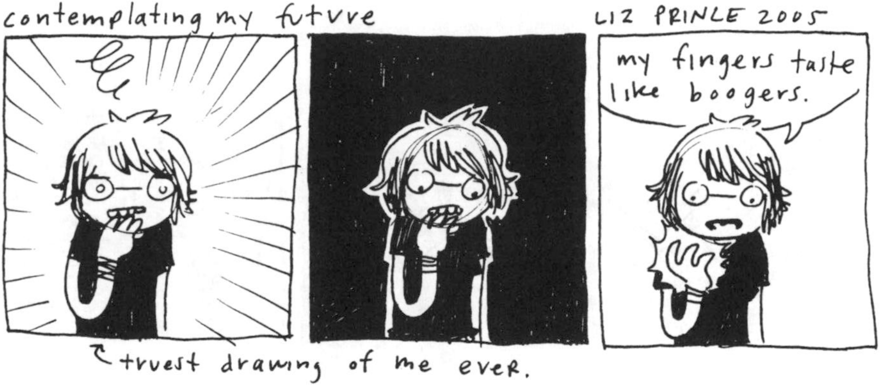
contemplating my future
LIZ PRINCE 2005
my fingers taste like boogers.
truest drawing of me ever.

Frog socks

LIZ PRINCE 2005

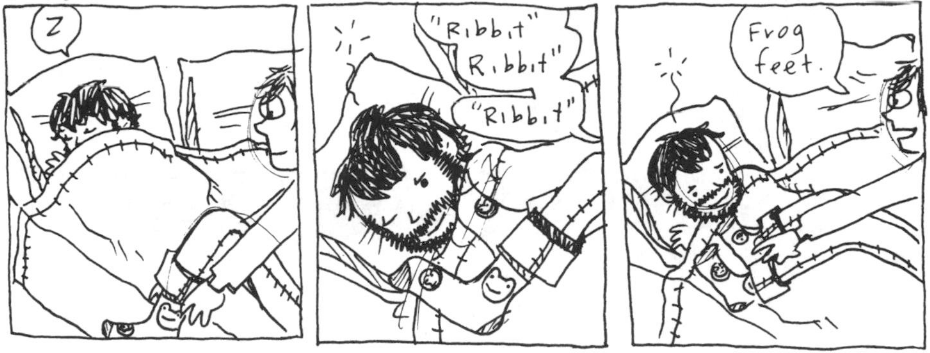
Z
"Ribbit"
"Ribbit"
"Ribbit"
Frog feet.

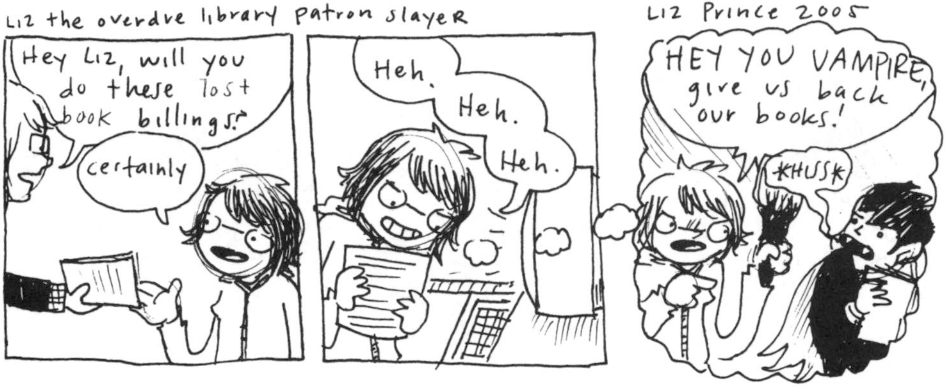
Liz the overdue library patron slayer
Liz Prince 2005
Hey Liz, will you do these lost book billings?
certainly
Heh.
Heh.
Heh.
HEY YOU VAMPIRE, give us back our books!
HUSK

a world of smiles for your mouth

LIZ PRINCE 2005

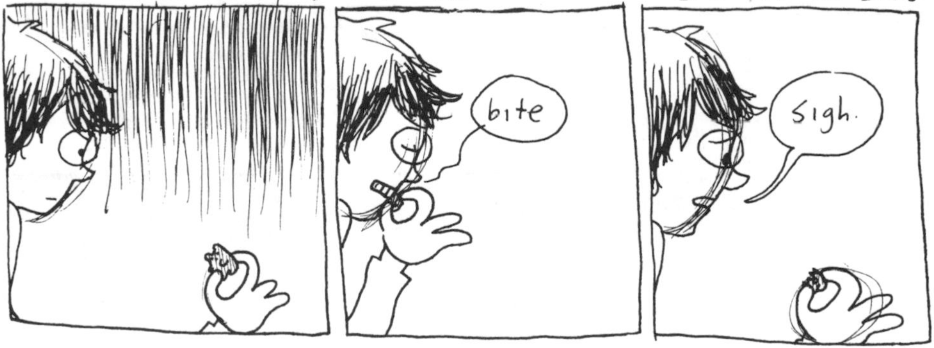
bite
sigh.

life imitates art

LIZ PRINCE 2005

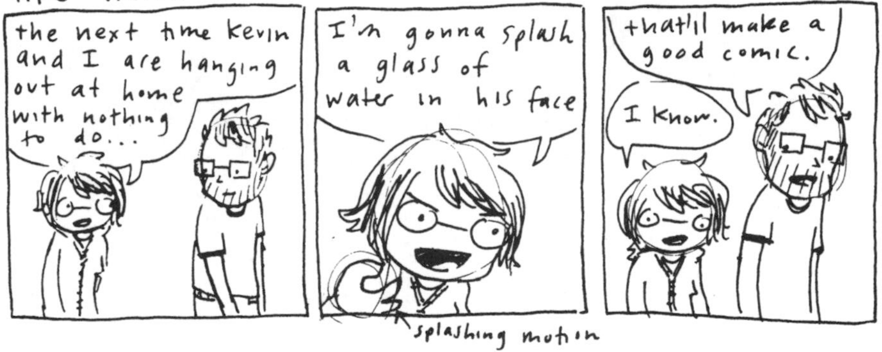
the next time kevin and I are hanging out at home with nothing to do...
I'm gonna splash a glass of water in his face
splashing motion
that'll make a good comic.
I know.

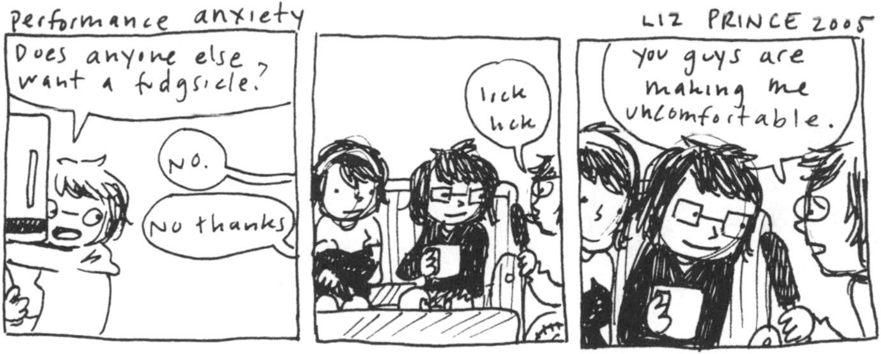
performance anxiety
LIZ PRINCE 2005
Does anyone else want a fudgsicle?
NO.
No thanks
lick lick
you guys are making me uncomfortable.

my new favorrite novelty flavour

LIZ PRINCE 2005

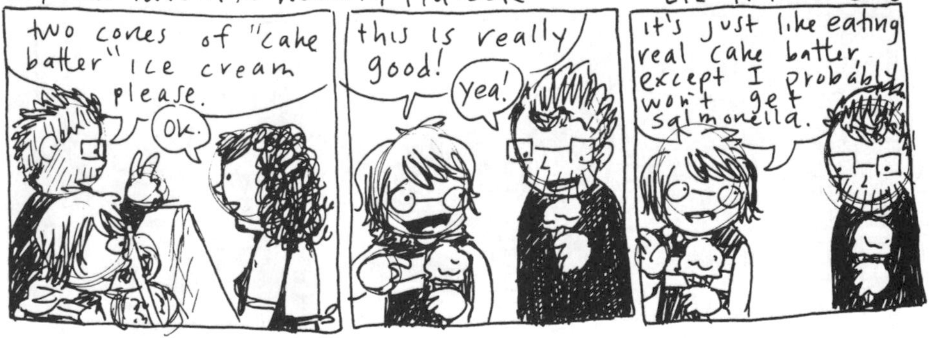
two cones of "cake batter" ice cream please.
Ok.
this is really good!
yea!
it's just like eating real cake batter, except I probably won't get salmonella.

Liz Prince gets shit done

LIZ PRINCE 2005

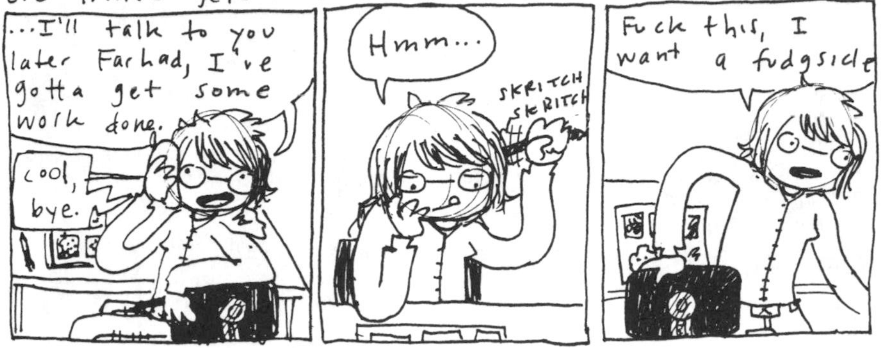
...I'll talk to you later Farhad, I've gotta get some work done.
cool, bye.
Hmm...
SKRITCH SKRITCH
Fuck this, I want a fudgsicle

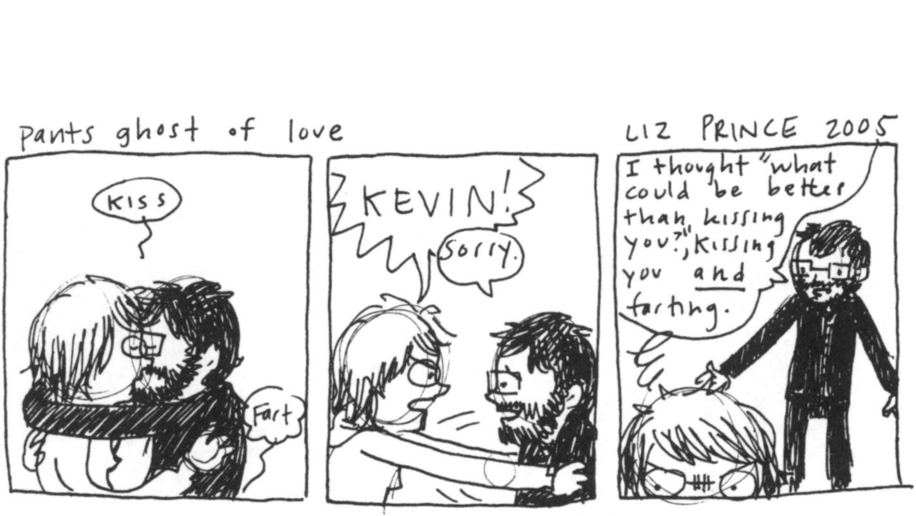
pants ghost of love
LIZ PRINCE 2005
KISS
Fart
KEVIN!
Sorry.
I thought "what could be better than kissing you?", kissing you and farting.

levi's store

LIZ PRINCE 2005

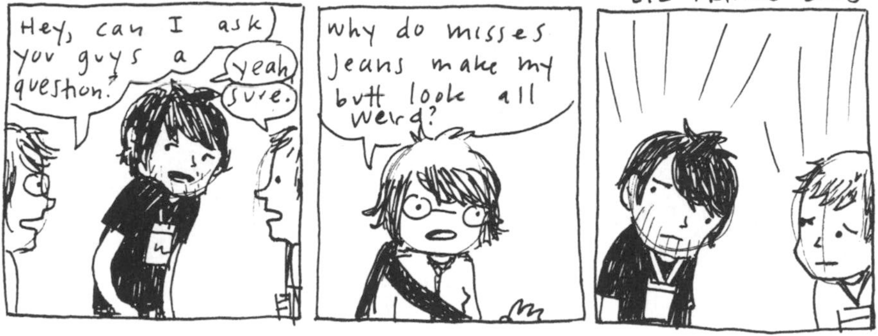
Hey, can I ask you guys a question?
yeah
sure.
why do misses jeans make my butt look all weird?

a hairy situation

LIZ PRINCE 2005

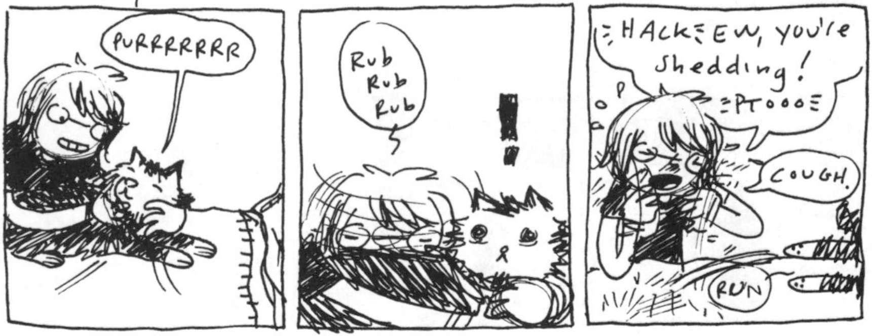
PURRRRRRR
Rub Rub Rub
HACK EW, you're shedding!
PTOOO
COUGH.
RUN

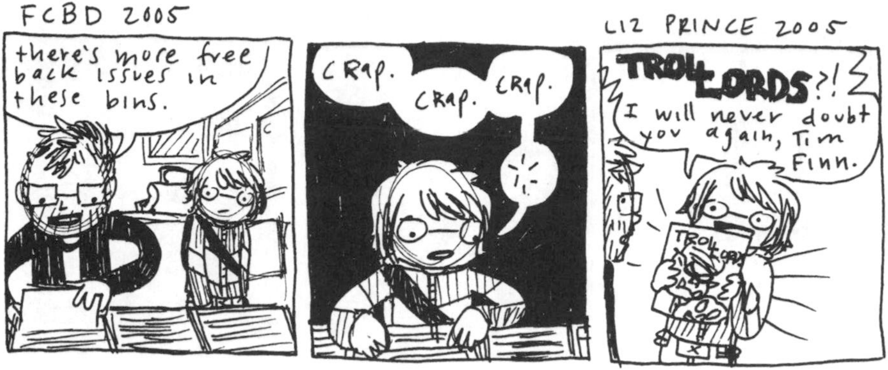
FCBD 2005
LIZ PRINCE 2005
there's more free back issues in these bins.
CRAP.
CRAP.
CRAP.
TROLLORDS?!
I will never doubt you again, Tim Finn.

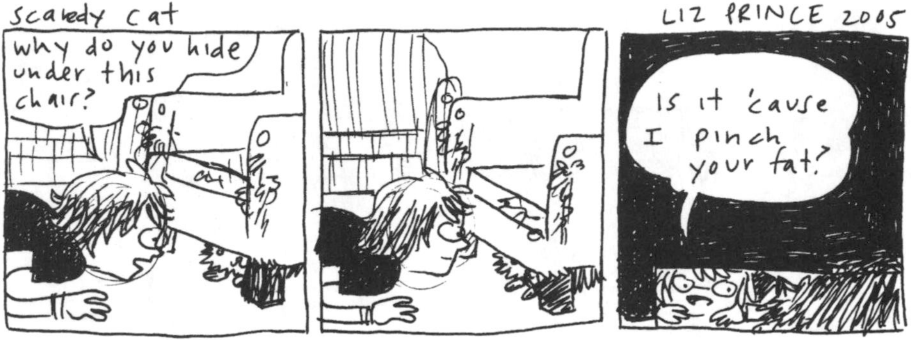
scaredy cat
LIZ PRINCE 2005
why do you hide under this chair?
Is it 'cause I pinch your fat?

kids these days

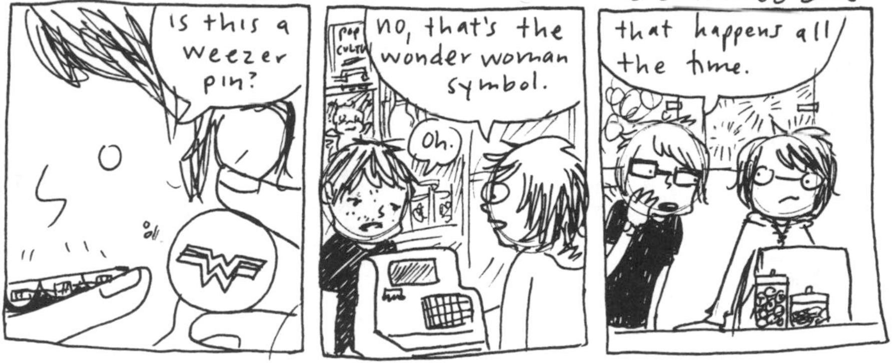
LIZ PRINCE 2005
is this a weezer pin?
no, that's the wonder woman symbol.
Oh.
that happens all the time.

Farhad's fuckin' funny.

LIZ PRINCE 2005

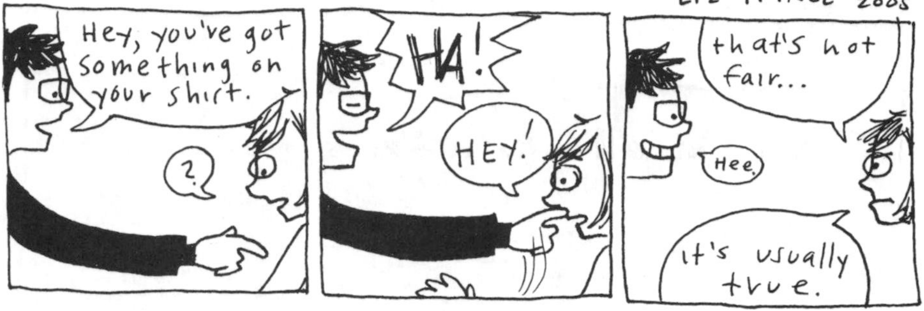
Hey, you've got something on your shirt.
?
HA!
HEY!
that's not fair...
Hee.
it's usually true.

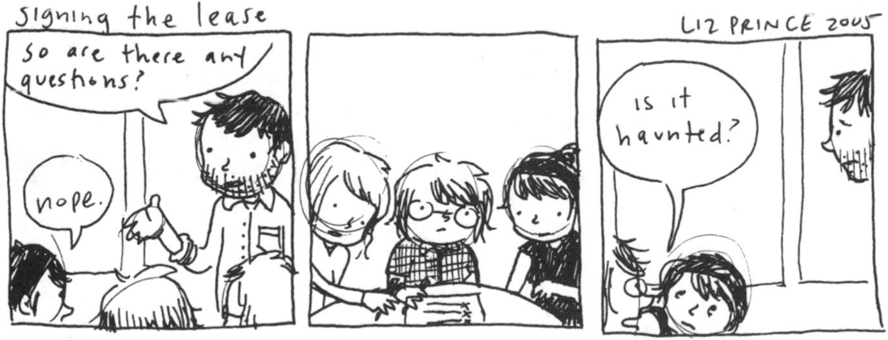
signing the lease
LIZ PRINCE 2005
so are there any questions?
nope.
is it haunted?

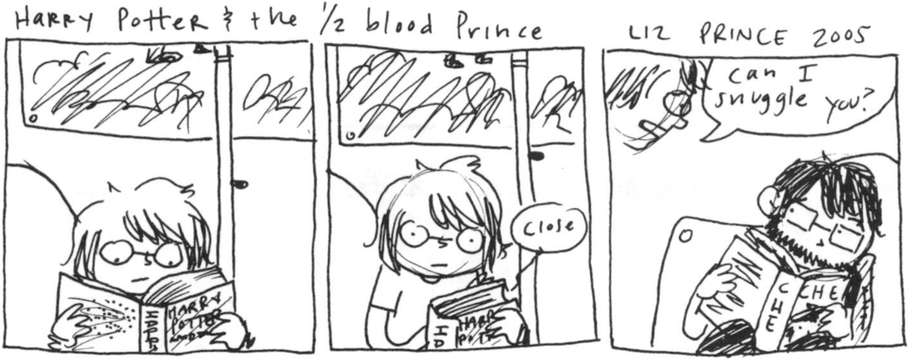
Harry Potter & the 1/2 blood Prince
LIZ PRINCE 2005
close
can I snuggle you?

terror of the Bees

LIZ PRINCE 2005

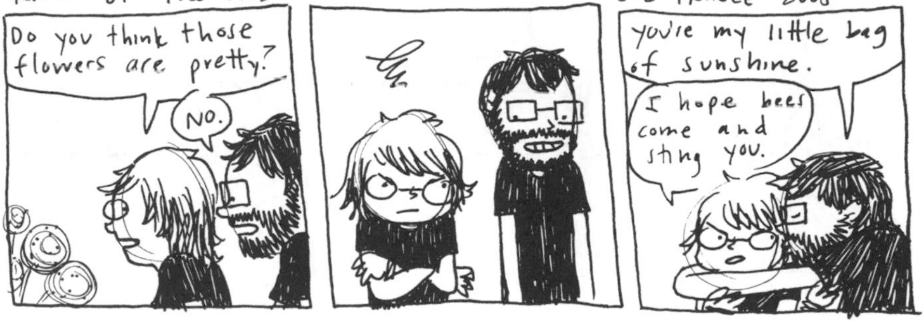
Do you think those flowers are pretty?
NO.
you're my little bag of sunshine.
I hope bees come and sting you.

birds and bees

LIZ PRINCE 2005

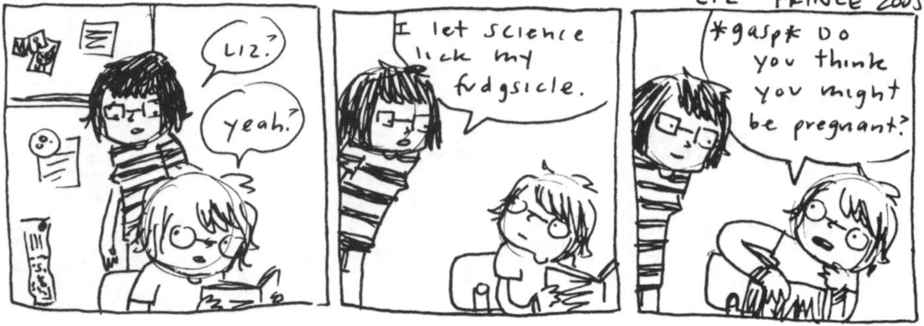
LIZ?
yeah?
I let science lick my fudgsicle.
gasp Do you think you might be pregnant?

Home Improvement

Liz Prince 2005

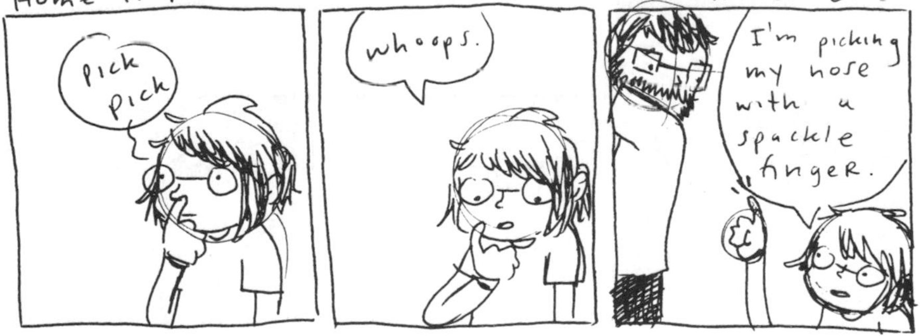

pick pick
whoops.
I'm picking my nose with a spackle finger.

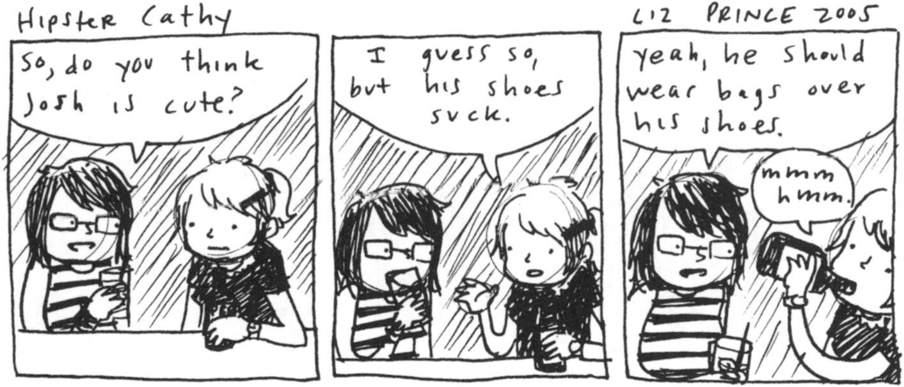
Hipster Cathy
LIZ PRINCE 2005
So, do you think Josh is cute?
I guess so, but his shoes suck.
yeah, he should wear bags over his shoes.
mmm hmm.

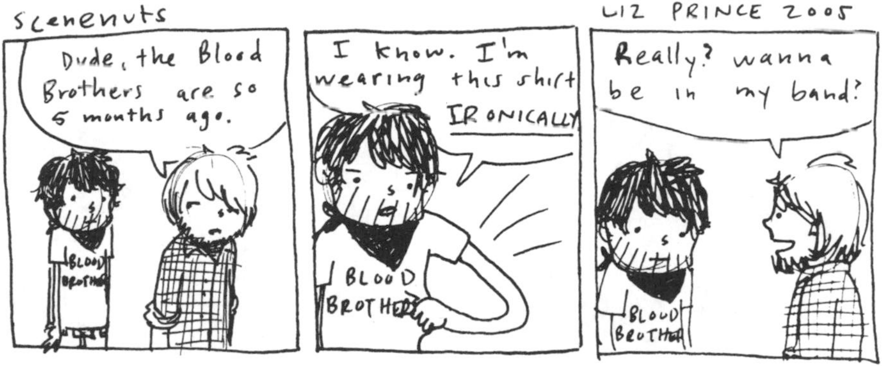
Scenenuts
LIZ PRINCE 2005
Dude, the Blood Brothers are so 5 months ago.
BLOOD BROTHER
I know. I'm wearing this shirt IRONICALLY
BLOOD BROTHER
Really? wanna be in my band?
BLOOD BROTHER

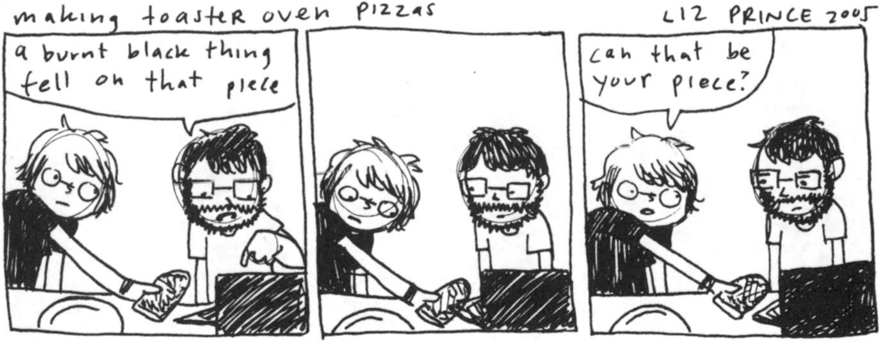
making toaster oven pizzas
LIZ PRINCE 2005
a burnt black thing fell on that piece
can that be your piece?

Geography

LIZ PRINCE 2005

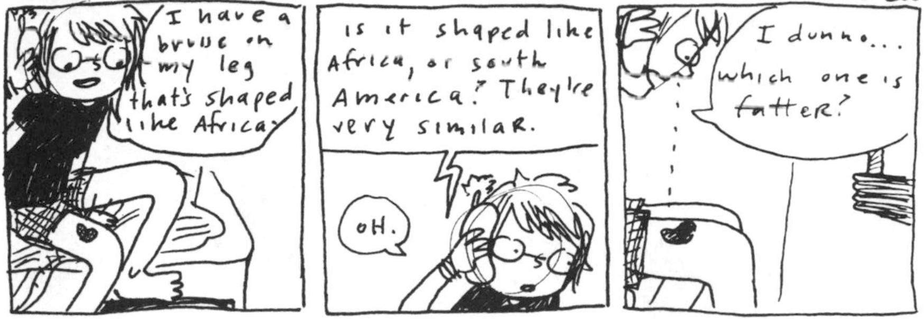
I have a bruise on my leg that's shaped like Africa
is it shaped like Africa, or south America? They're very similar.
OH.
I dunno... which one is fatter?

Never believe your own press

LIZ PRINCE 2005

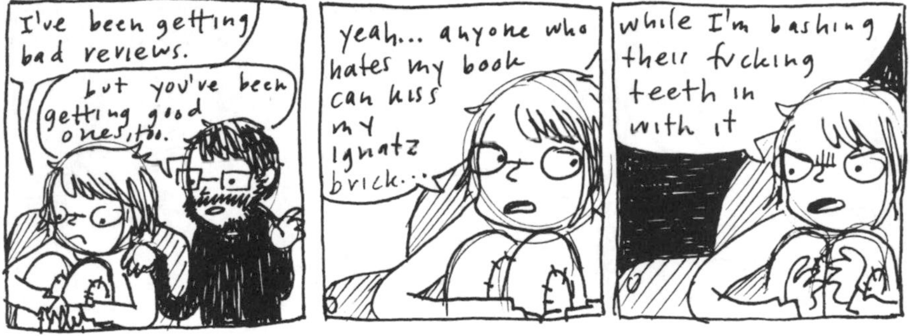
I've been getting bad reviews.
but you've been getting good ones, too.
yeah... anyone who hates my book can kiss my Ignatz brick...
while I'm bashing their fucking teeth in with it

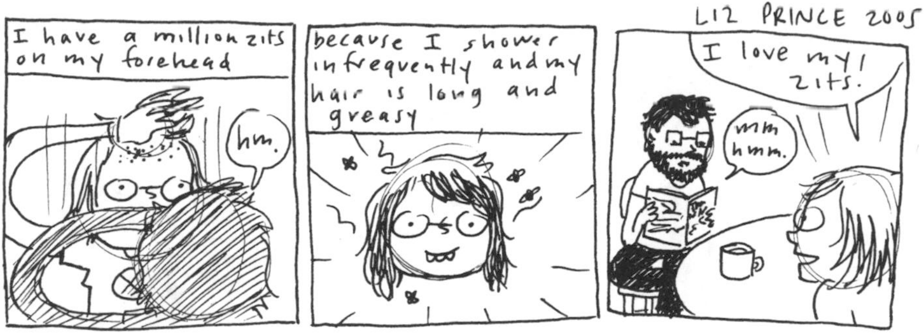
I have a million zits on my forehead
hm.
because I shower infrequently and my hair is long and greasy
LIZ PRINCE 2005
I love my! zits.
mm hmm.

Dry my eyes

LIZ PRINCE 2006

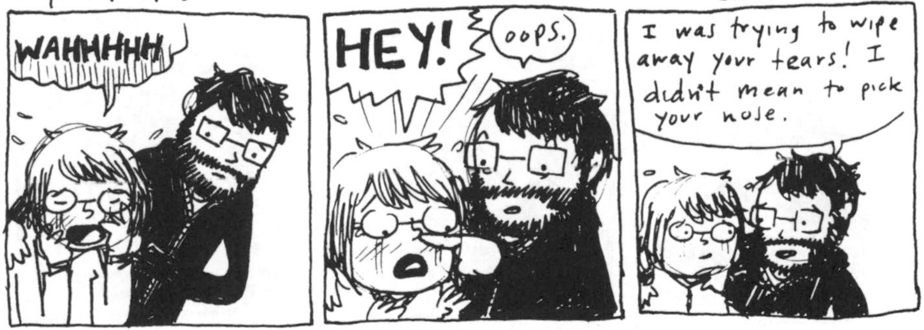
WAHHHHH
HEY!
oops.
I was trying to wipe away your tears! I didn't mean to pick your nose.

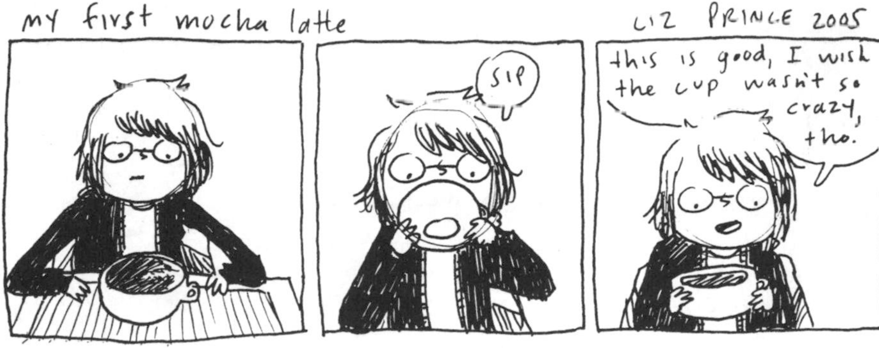
my first mocha latte
LIZ PRINCE 2005
SIP
this is good, I wish the cup wasn't so crazy, tho.

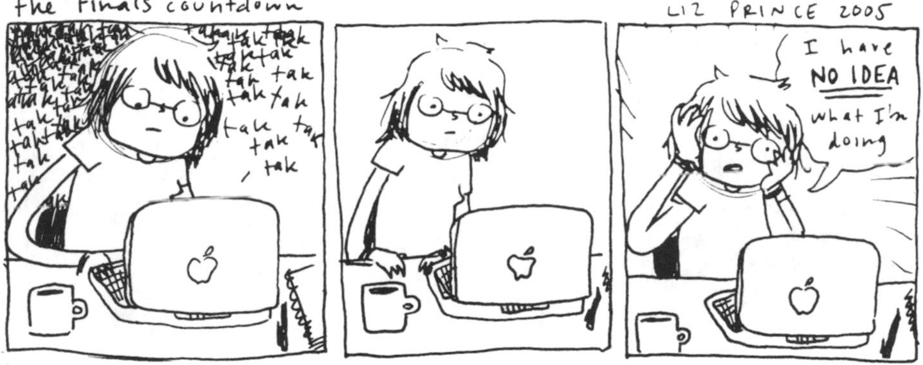
the Finals countdown
LIZ PRINCE 2005
tak tak tak tak tak
I have NO IDEA what I'm doing

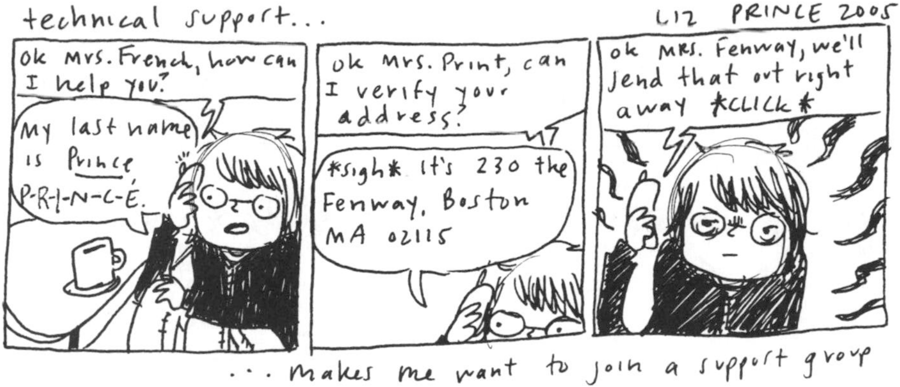
technical support...
LIZ PRINCE 2005
ok Mrs. French, how can I help you?
My last name is Prince, P-R-I-N-C-E.
ok Mrs. Print, can I verify your address?
sigh It's 230 the Fenway, Boston MA 02115
ok MRS. Fenway, we'll send that out right away *CLICK*
...makes me want to join a support group

the power of pussy beer

LIZ PRINCE 2006

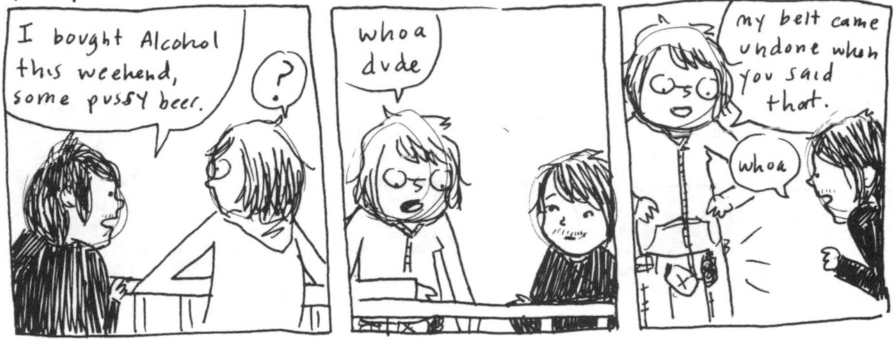
I bought Alcohol this weekend, some pussy beer.
?
whoa dude
my belt came undone when you said that.
whoa

my tummy hurts because I'm nervous

LIZ PRINCE 2006

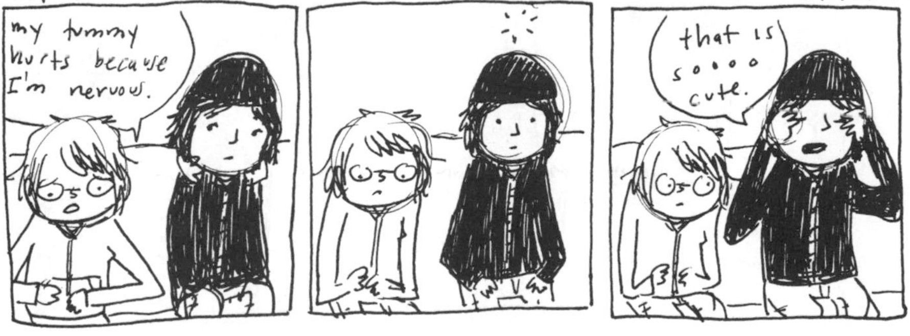

my tummy hurts because I'm nervous.
that is soooo cute.

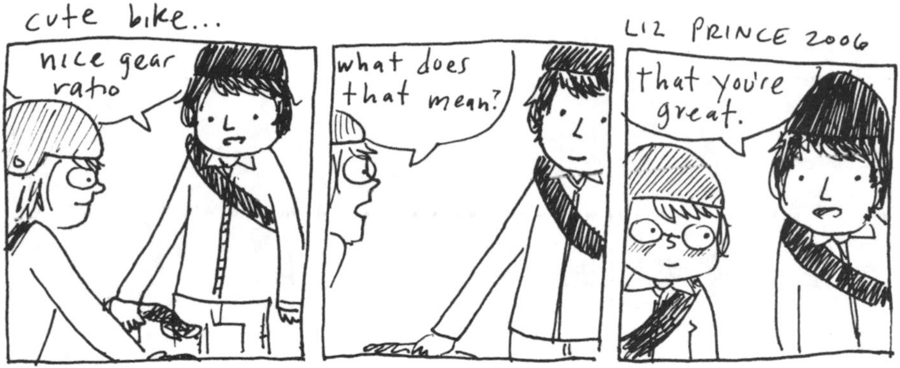
cute bike...
nice gear ratio
what does that mean?
LIZ PRINCE 2006
that you're great.

sneezes on a plane

LIZ PRINCE 2006

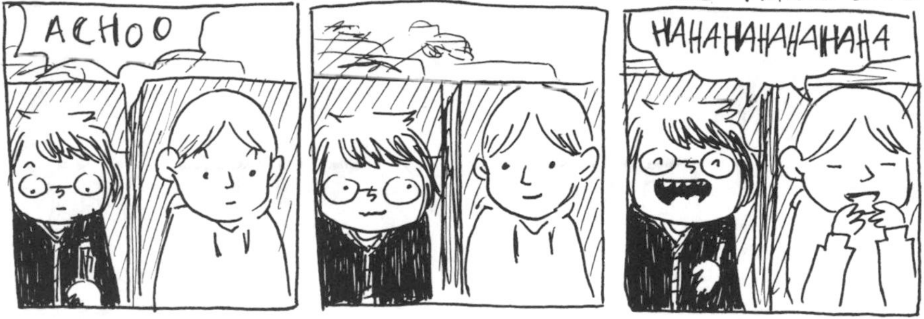
ACHOO
HAHAHAHAHAHAHAHA

kissing Kaz in the abandoned apartment
next to Aaron's after A.P.E.

LIZ PRINCE 2006

can I kiss you now?

yes.

so... do you like dorky guys?

the cat's meow

LIZ PRINCE 2006

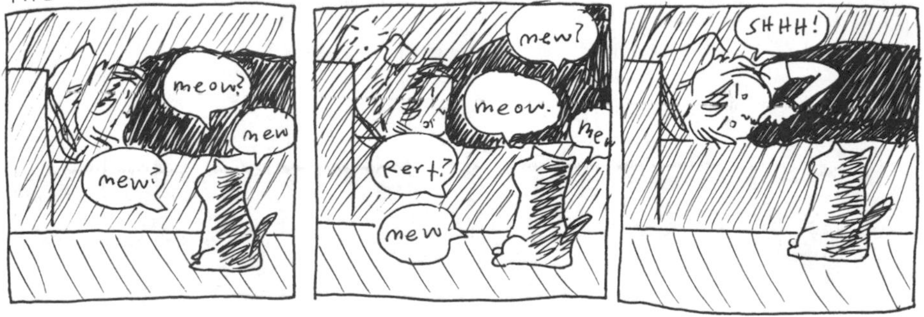
meow?
mew
mew?
mew?
meow.
mew
Rert?
mew
SHHH!

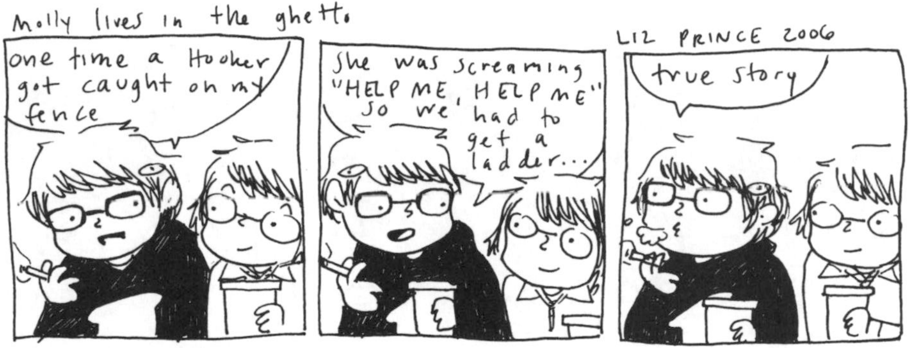
Molly lives in the ghetto
LIZ PRINCE 2006
one time a Hooker got caught on my fence
She was screaming "HELP ME, HELP ME" so we had to get a ladder...
true story

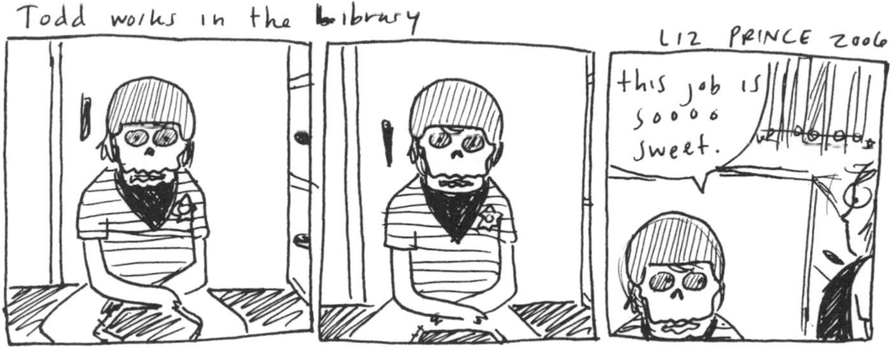
Todd works in the library
LIZ PRINCE 2006
this job is soooo sweet.

I am a minor celebrity LIZ PRINCE 2006

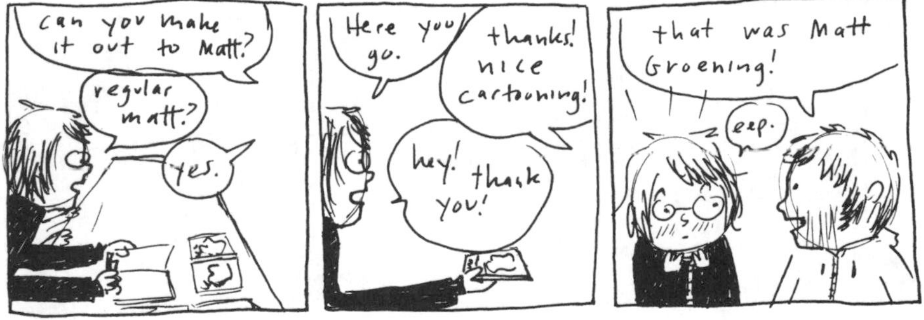
can you make it out to Matt?
regular matt?
yes.
Here you go.
thanks! nice cartooning!
hey! thank you!
that was Matt Groening!
eep.

NOTHING

LIZ PRINCE 2006

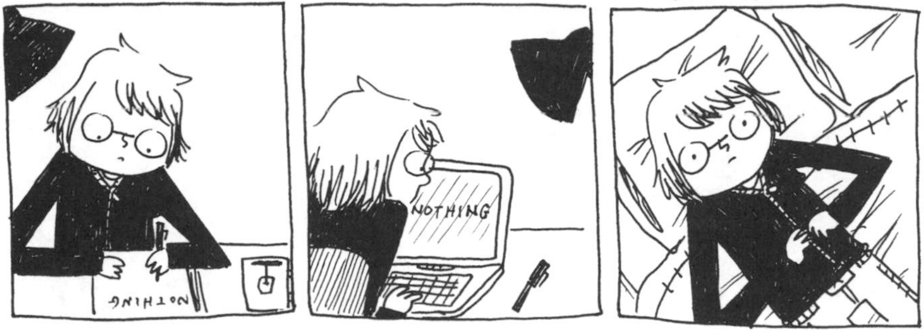
NOTHING
NOTHING

"the idiot" by LIZ PRINCE

LIZ PRINCE 2006

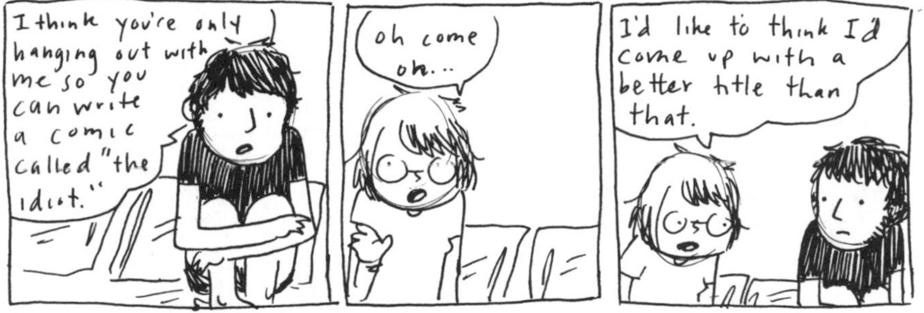
I think you're only hanging out with me so you can write a comic called "the idiot."
oh come on...
I'd like to think I'd come up with a better title than that.

cookie dough legs

LIZ PRINCE 2006

ugh, I have cookie dough legs.

you mean your legs feel like cookie dough?

No. they feel like I've been eating cookie dough all day.

Skivvy dipping

LIZ PRINCE 2006

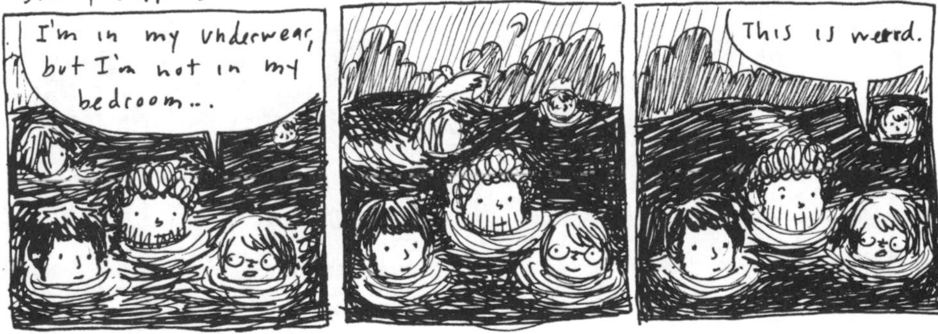
I'm in my underwear, but I'm not in my bedroom...
This is weird.

Don't eat the ducks

LIZ PRINCE 2006

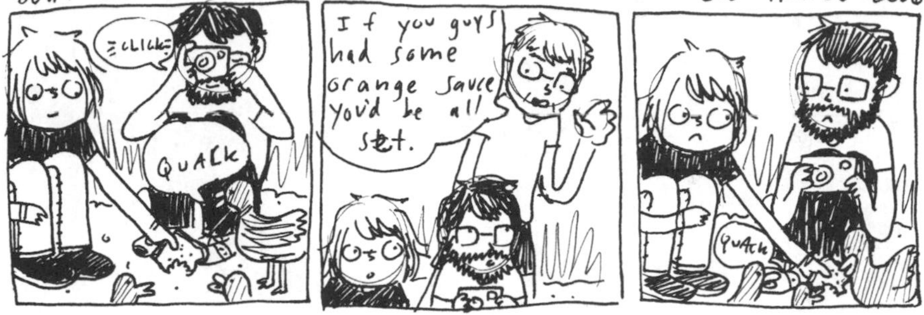
CLICK
QUACK
If you guys had some orange sauce you'd be all set.
QUACK

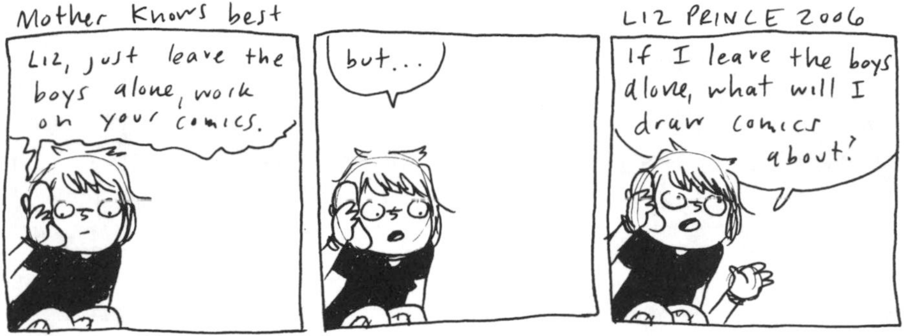
Mother Knows best
LIZ PRINCE 2006
Liz, just leave the boys alone, work on your comics.
but...
If I leave the boys alone, what will I draw comics about?

Lifesaver

LIZ PRINCE 2006

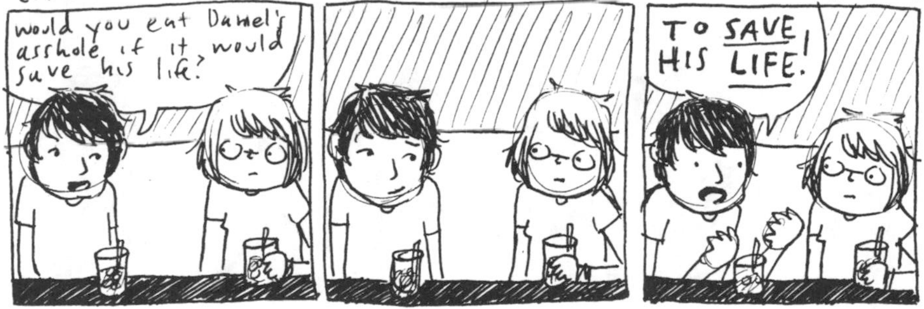
would you eat Daniel's asshole if it would save his life?
TO SAVE HIS LIFE!

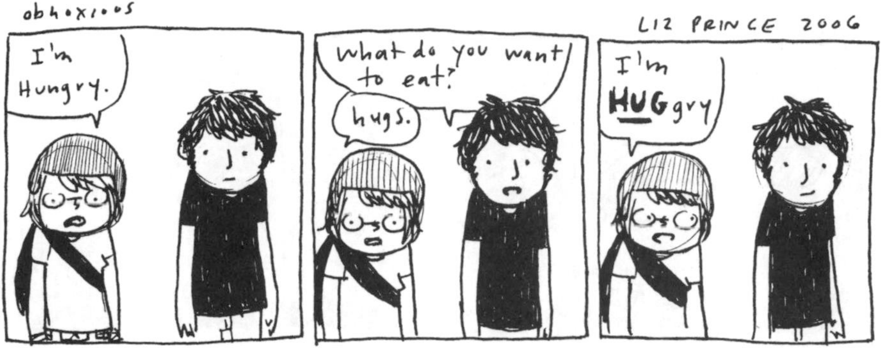
obnoxious
LIZ PRINCE 2006
I'm Hungry.
What do you want to eat?
hugs.
I'm HUGgry

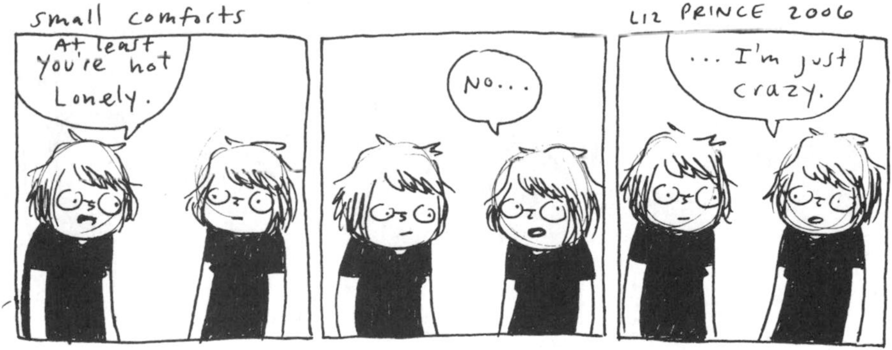
small comforts
LIZ PRINCE 2006
At least you're not Lonely.
No...
... I'm just crazy.

Zac Scheinbaum: Library Patron

LIZ PRINCE 2004

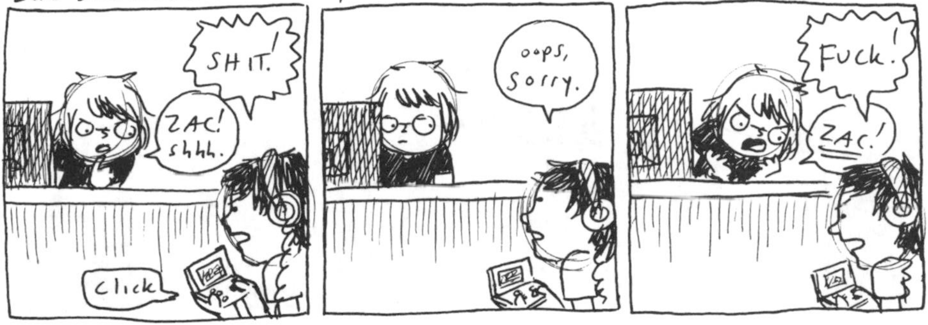
SHIT!
ZAC! shhh.
click
oops, sorry.
FUCK!
ZAC!

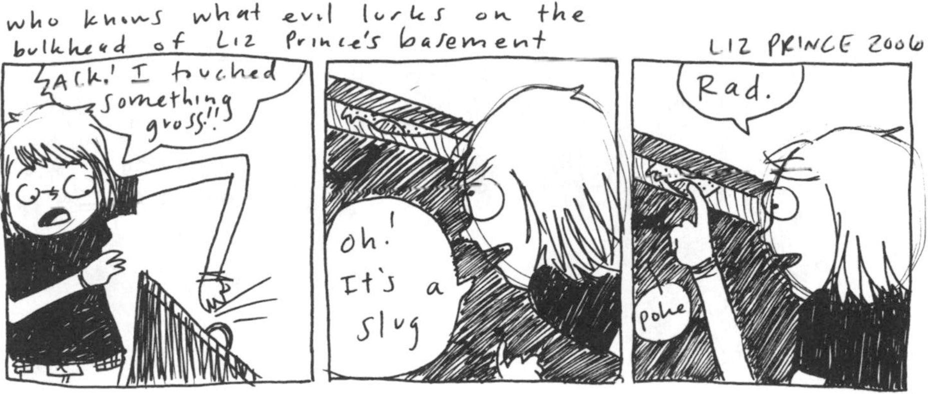
who knows what evil lurks on the bulkhead of Liz Prince's basement
LIZ PRINCE 2006
ACK! I touched something gross!!
Oh! It's a slug
Rad.
poke

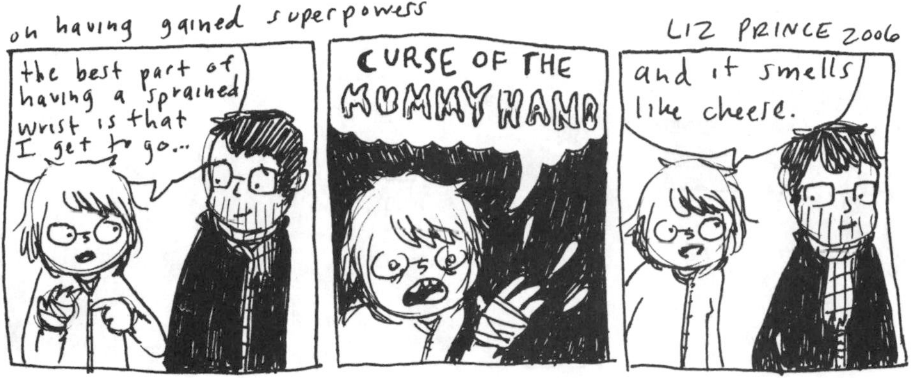
on having gained superpowers
LIZ PRINCE 2006
the best part of having a sprained wrist is that I get to go...
CURSE OF THE MUMMY HAND
and it smells like cheese.

zac's new tattoo

LIZ PRINCE 2006

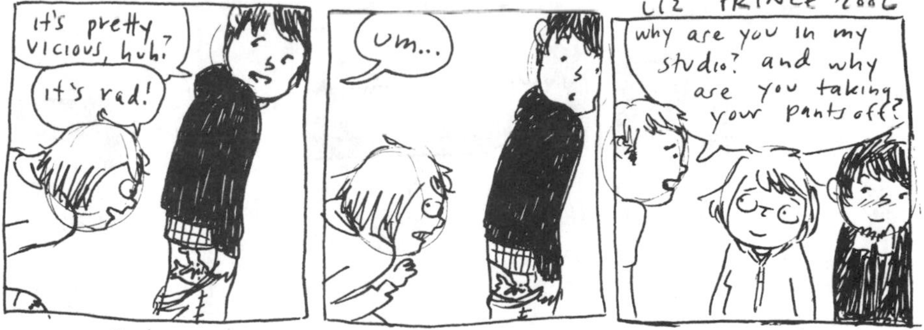
it's pretty vicious, huh?
it's rad!
um...
why are you in my studio? and why are you taking your pants off?

(it's a giant squid fighting a whale)

as O.D.B. would say, "You don't want to fuck with me" LIZ PRINCE 2006

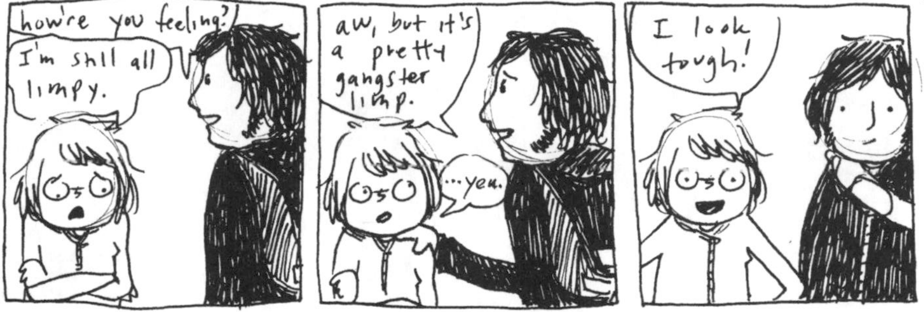
how're you feeling?
I'm still all limpy.
aw, but it's a pretty gangster limp.
...yea.
I look tough!

smash the state

LIZ PRINCE 2006

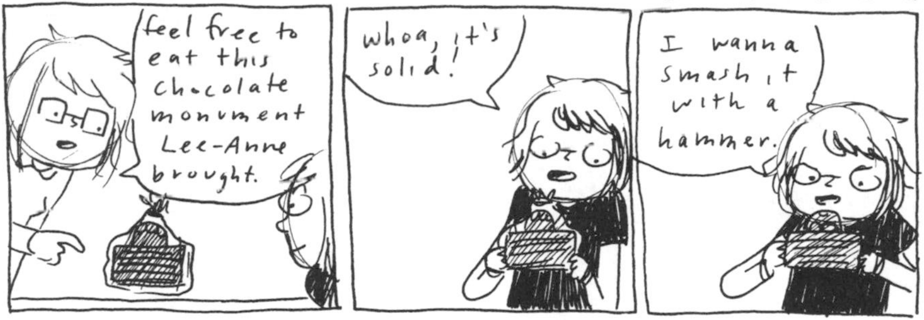

feel free to eat this chocolate monument Lee-Anne brought.
whoa, it's solid!
I wanna smash it with a hammer.

Guitar Zero

LIZ PRINCE 2006

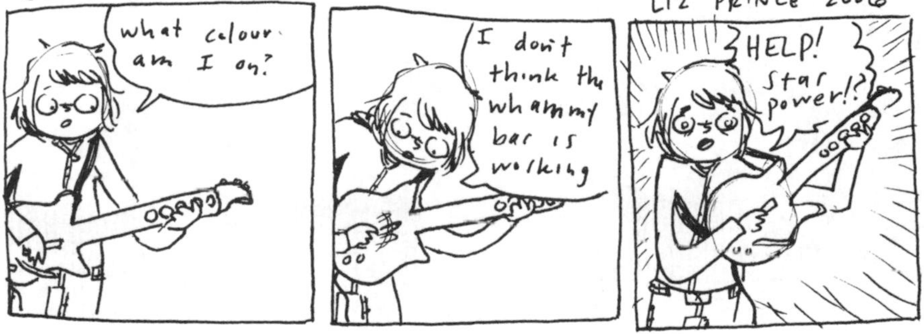
what colour am I on?
I don't think the whammy bar is working
HELP! Star power!?

Guitar Hero 2

LIZ PRINCE 2006

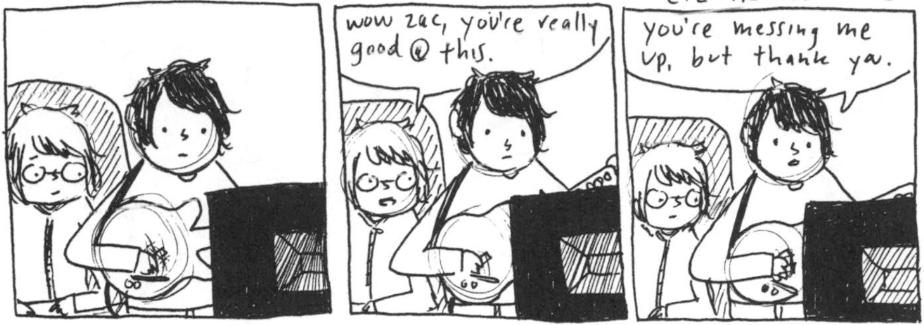
wow zac, you're really good @ this.
you're messing me up, but thank you.

on the bright side

LIZ PRINCE 2006

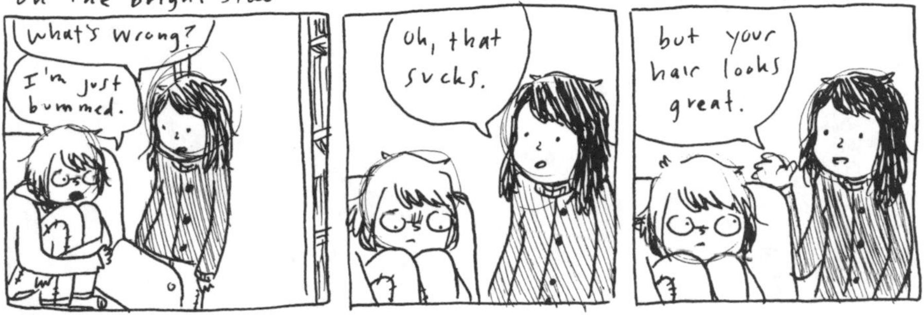

what's wrong?
I'm just bummed.
Oh, that sucks.
but your hair looks great.

creative process

LIZ PRINCE 2006

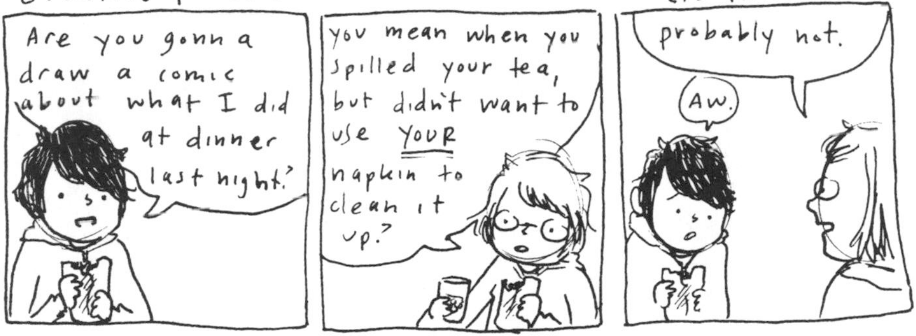
Are you gonna draw a comic about what I did at dinner last night?
you mean when you spilled your tea, but didn't want to use YOUR napkin to clean it up?
probably not.
AW.

OUI

LIZ PRINCE 2007

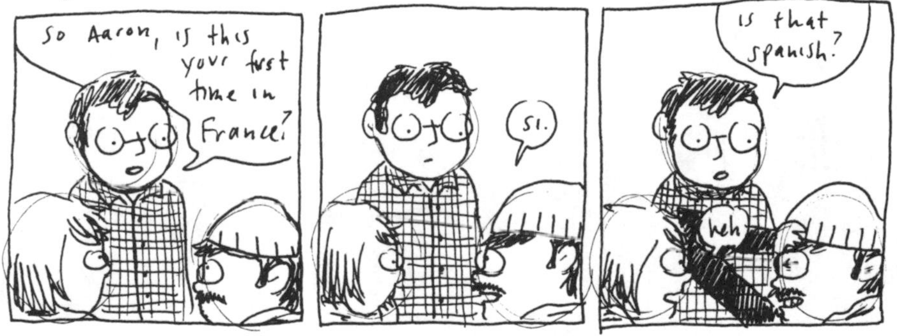

So Aaron, is this your first time in France?
Si.
Is that spanish?
heh

Doug Harry: former vegan

LIZ PRINCE 2007

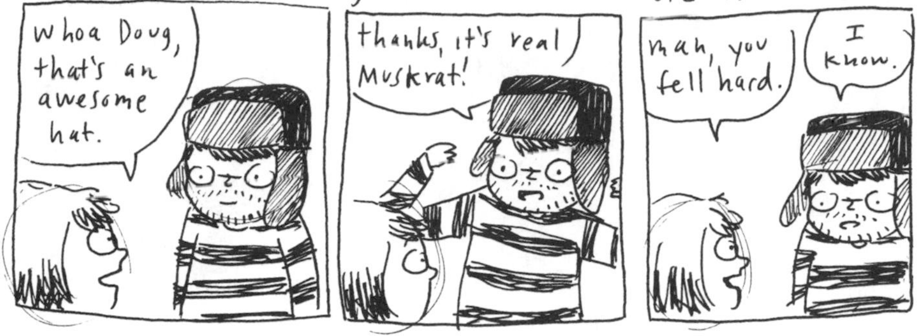
whoa Doug, that's an awesome hat.
thanks, it's real Muskrat!
man, you fell hard.
I know.

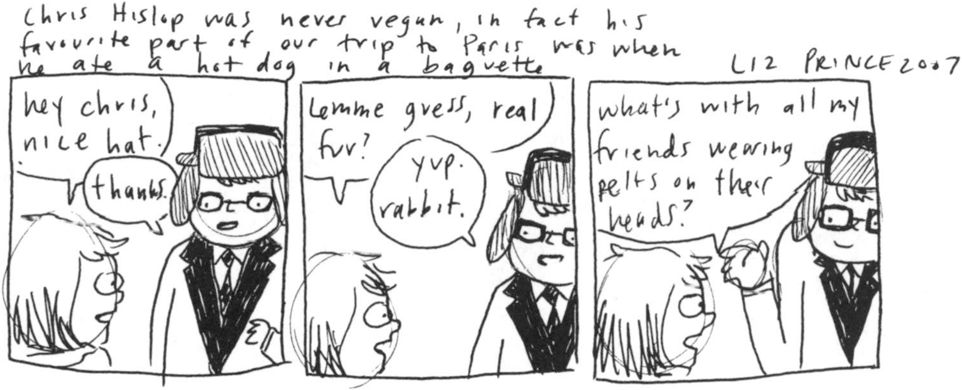
Chris Hislop was never vegan, in fact his favourite part of our trip to Paris was when he ate a hot dog in a baguette
LIZ PRINCE 2007
hey chris, nice hat.
thanks.
lemme guess, real fur?
yup. rabbit.
what's with all my friends wearing pelts on their heads?

Liz Prince: practicing vegetarian

Liz Prince 2007

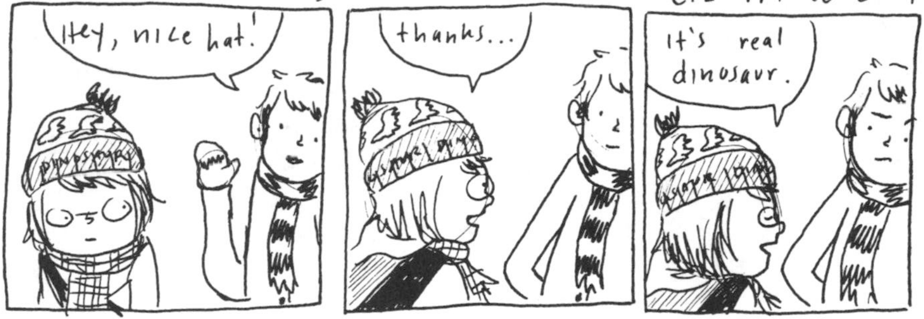
Hey, nice hat!
thanks...
It's real dinosaur.

Hungry like the wolf

LIZ PRINCE 2007

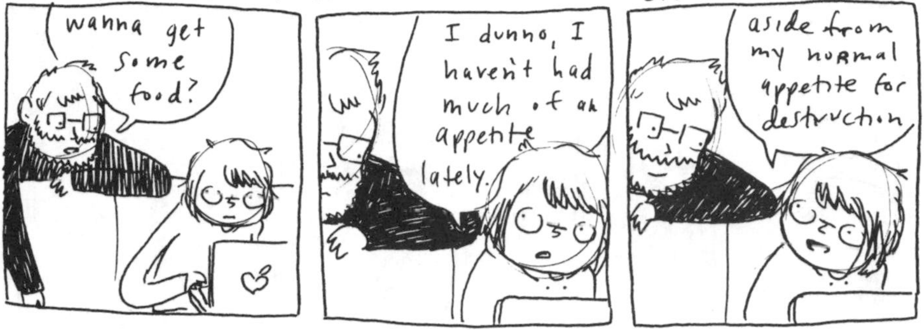
wanna get some food?
I dunno, I haven't had much of an appetite lately.
aside from my normal appetite for destruction

morning pick-me-up

LIZ PRINCE 2007

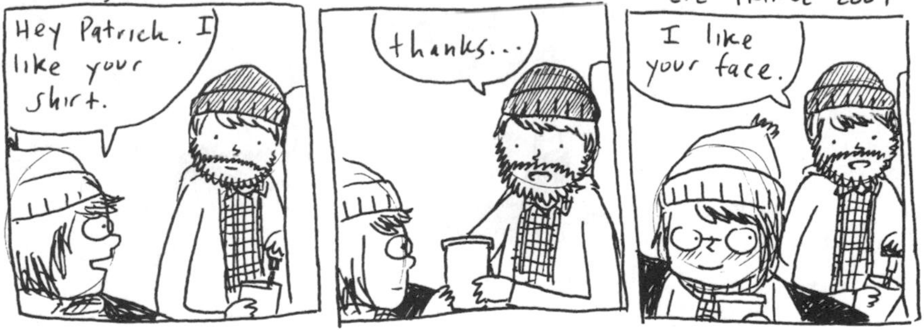
Hey Patrick. I like your shirt.
thanks...
I like your face.

my sources say "fuck you"

LIZ PRINCE 2007

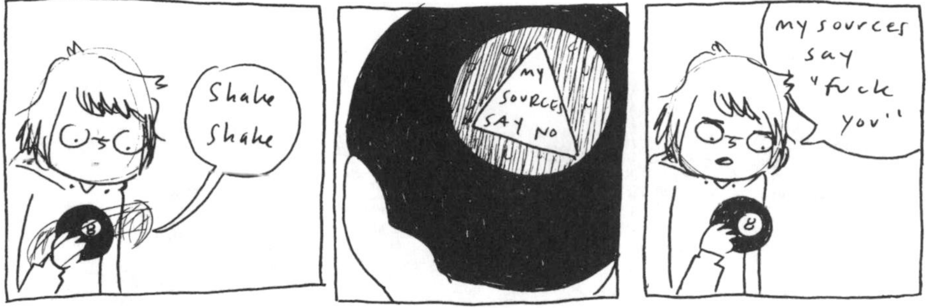
Shake Shake
MY SOURCES SAY NO
my sources say "fuck you"

Naveed's massive headwound

LIZ PRINCE 2007

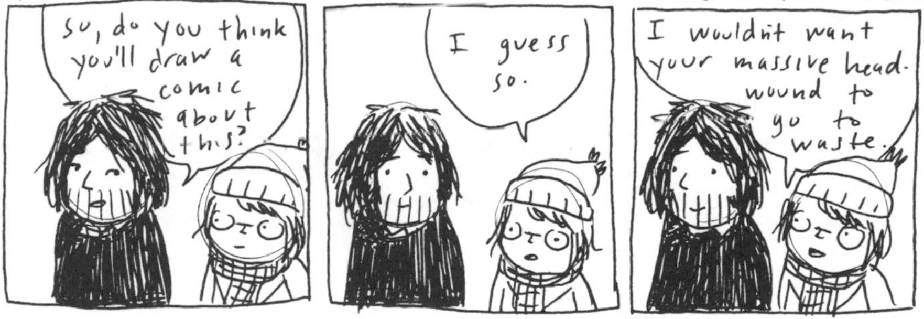
so, do you think you'll draw a comic about this?
I guess so.
I wouldn't want your massive head-wound to go to waste.

my empowering sense of humour

Liz Prince 2007

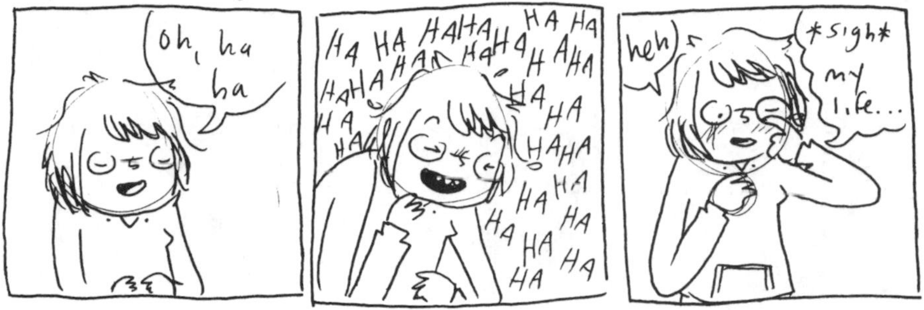
Oh, ha ha
HA HA HAHA HA HA HA HA HAHA HA HA HA HA HA HA HAHA HA HA HA HAHA HA HA HA HA HA HA HA HA HA
heh
sigh my life...

Molly Bradbury's ego, circa 1999

LIZ PRINCE 2007

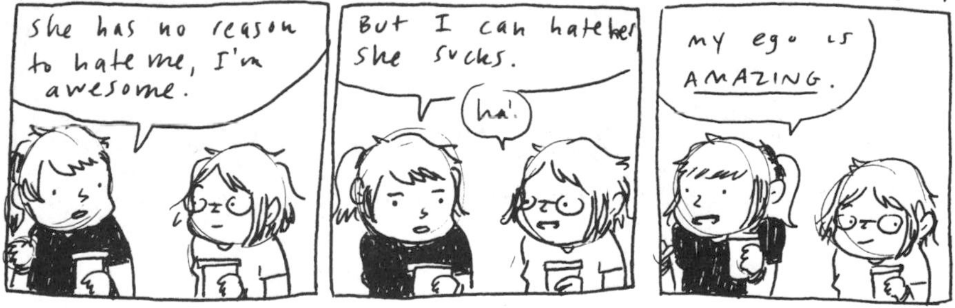

She has no reason to hate me, I'm awesome.
But I can hate her. She sucks.
ha!
my ego is AMAZING.

hip with the kids

LIZ PRINCE 2007

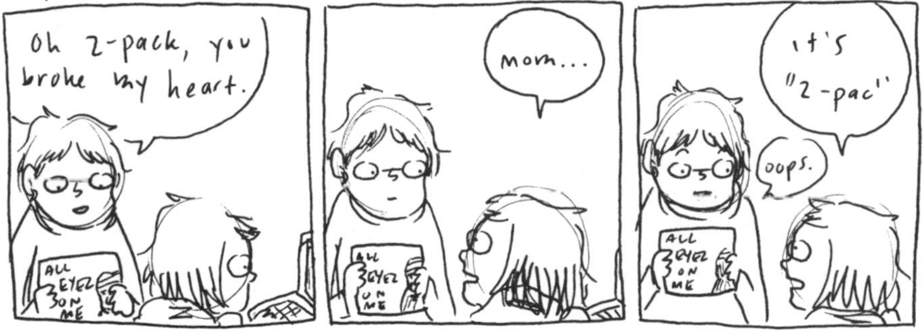
Oh 2-pack, you broke my heart.
ALL EYEZ ON ME
mom...
ALL EYEZ ON ME
it's "2-pac"
oops.
ALL EYEZ ON ME

prelude to a sinus infection

LIZ PRINCE 2007

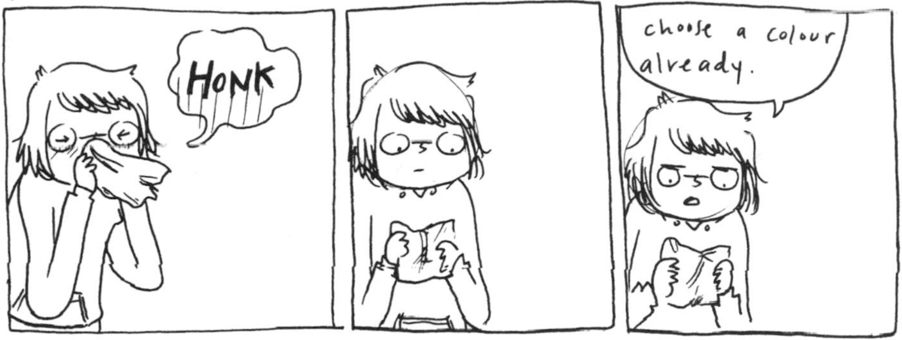
HONK
choose a colour already.

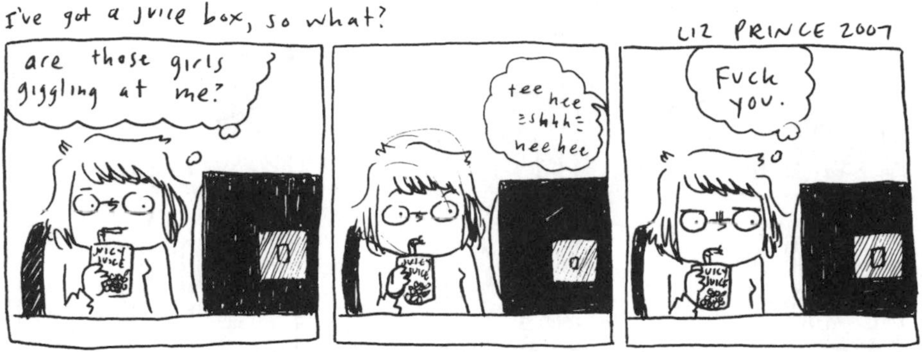
I've got a juice box, so what?
LIZ PRINCE 2007
are those girls giggling at me?
tee hee
shhh
hee hee
Fuck you.

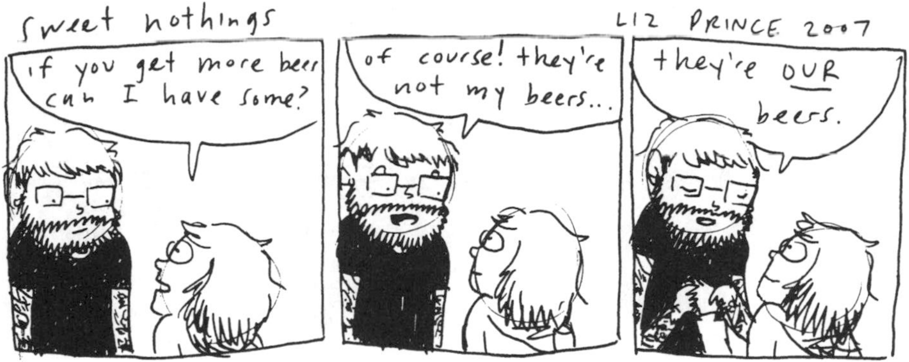
sweet nothings
LIZ PRINCE 2007
if you get more beer can I have some?
of course! they're not my beers...
they're OUR beers.

a better door than a window

LIZ PRINCE 2007

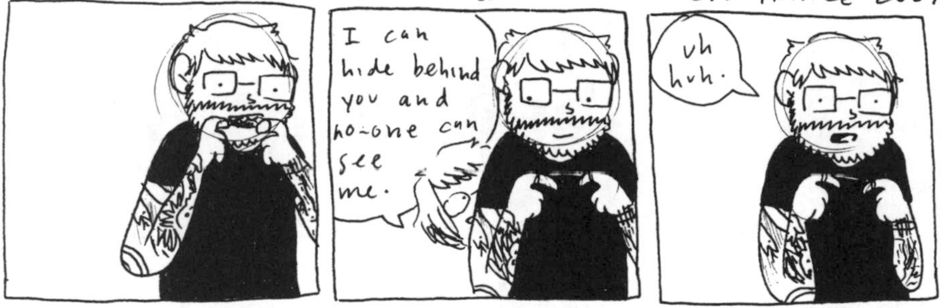
I can hide behind you and no-one can see me.
uh huh.

party tricks

LIZ PRINCE 2007

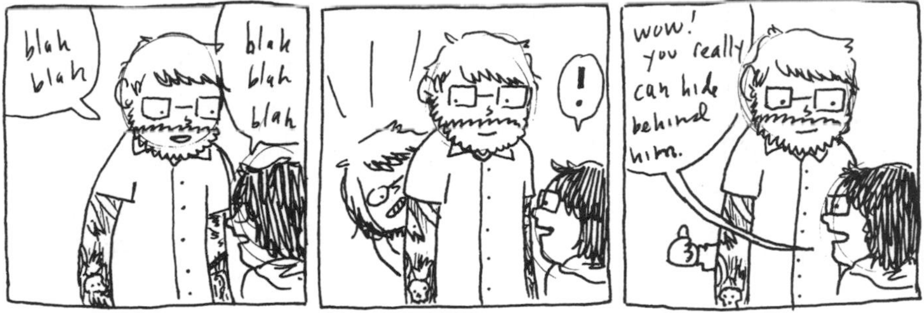

blah blah
blah blah blah
!
wow! you really can hide behind him.

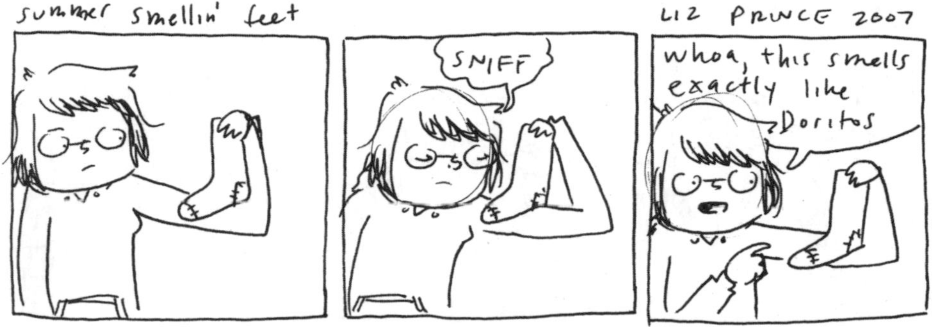
summer smellin' feet
LIZ PRINCE 2007
SNIFF
whoa, this smells exactly like Doritos

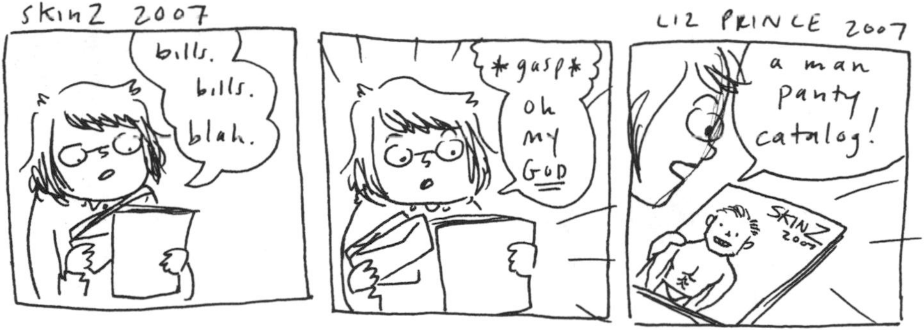
SKINZ 2007
bills.
bills.
blah.
gasp
oh my GOD
LIZ PRINCE 2007
a man panty catalog!
SKINZ 2007

Pillow talk

LIZ PRINCE 2007

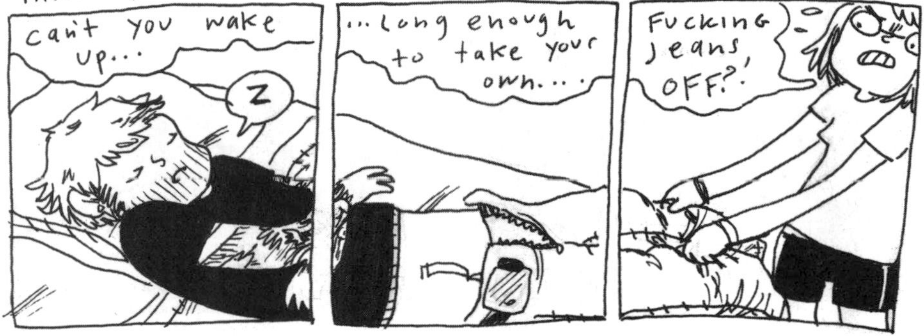

Can't you wake up...
Z
...long enough to take your own....
Fucking jeans, OFF?!

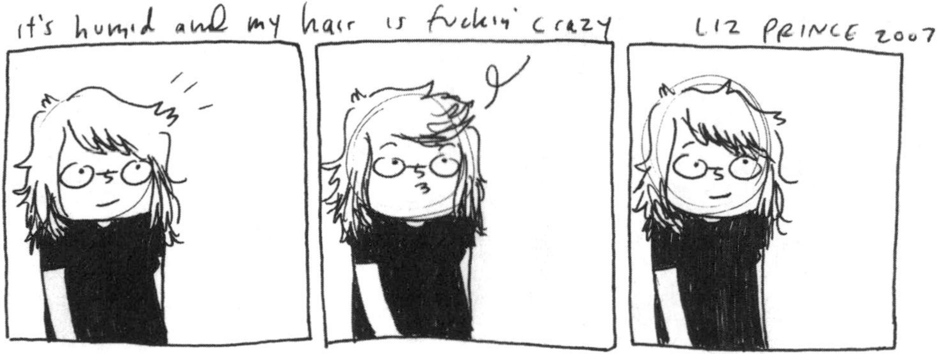
it's humid and my hair is fuckin' crazy
LIZ PRINCE 2007

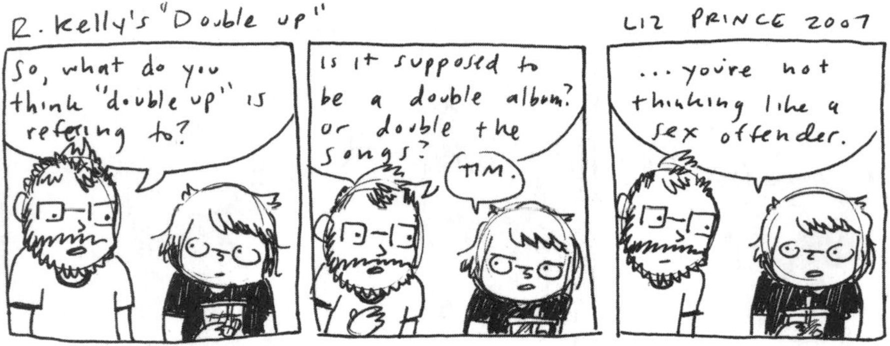
R. Kelly's "Double up"
LIZ PRINCE 2007
So, what do you think "double up" is refering to?
Is it supposed to be a double album? or double the songs?
TIM.
...you're not thinking like a sex offender.

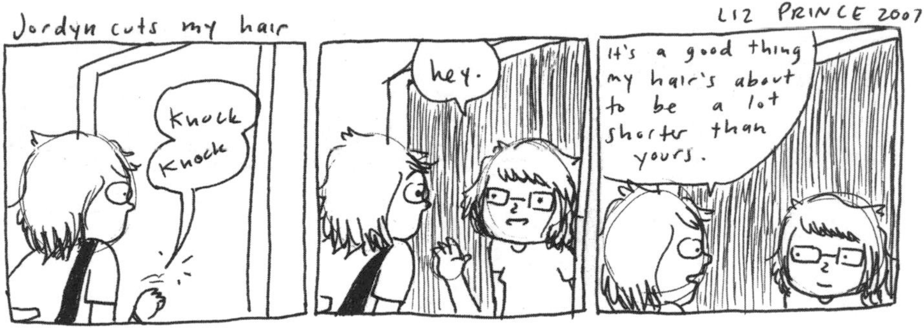
Jordyn cuts my hair
LIZ PRINCE 2007
Knock Knock
hey.
It's a good thing my hair's about to be a lot shorter than yours.

Pee-boy?

Liz Prince 2007

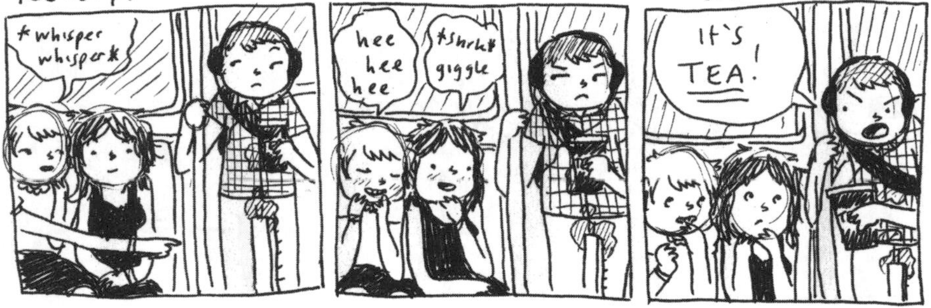
whisper whisper
hee hee hee
snrk giggle
It's TEA!

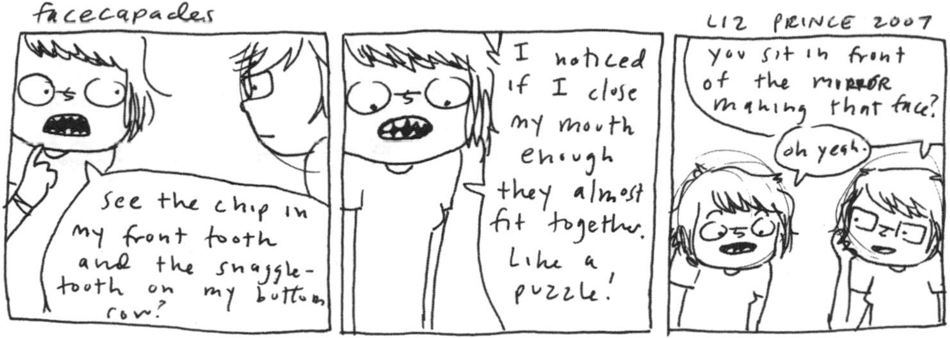
facecapades
LIZ PRINCE 2007
See the chip in my front tooth and the snaggle-tooth on my bottom row?
I noticed if I close my mouth enough they almost fit together. Like a puzzle!
you sit in front of the MIRROR making that face?
oh yeah.

Hell no, she won't go

LIZ PRINCE 2007

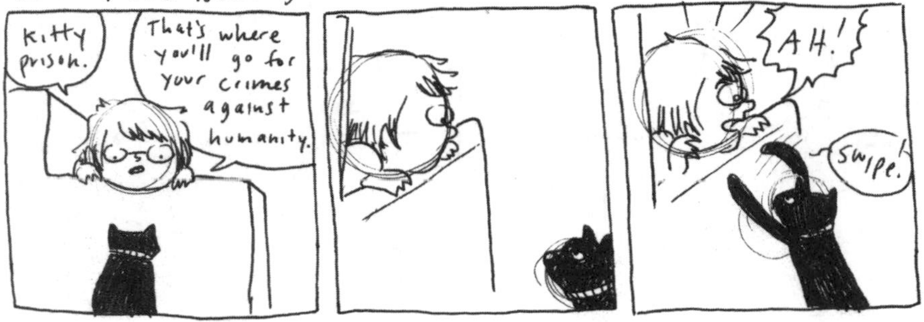
Kitty prison.
That's where you'll go for your crimes against humanity.
AH!
Swipe!

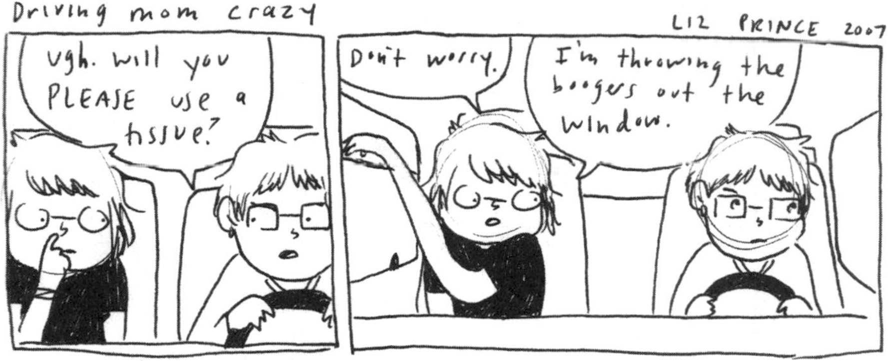
Driving mom crazy
LIZ PRINCE 2007
Ugh. Will you PLEASE use a tissue?
Don't worry.
I'm throwing the boogers out the window.

Liz Prince drinks coffee and draws comics in Somerville, MA. She enjoys mail!

p.o. box 441214
W. Somerville MA 02144
(preferred method)

lizprincepower @ hotmail.com
(accepted method)